S0-BYW-540

"Thank you, Christopher Lind, for sharing with us the vision of an economic order that is both moral and real; this is important food for thought for all Canadians."
— Ursula M. Franklin C.C. FRSC, University Professor Emerita, Toronto

"*Rumours of a Moral Economy* asks us to rethink our most fundamental assumptions about the economy. In this brave and intelligent book, Lind makes the case for moral economy as an intellectual discipline that recognizes that a market economy cannot be an autonomous and self-regulating entity. Moreover, to protect our deepest values and our planet, we must build a truly moral economy."
— Fred Block, Professor of Sociology, University of California at Davis

"Economics is called the dismal science, not because it's boring, but because it seems simply to glorify greed and to have no moral centre. Christopher Lind makes a compelling case for a moral economy where ethics has its rightful place. In the era of Goldman Sachs and BP this book is truly timely."
— Mel Watkins, Recipient of the John Kenneth Galbraith Award in Economics and Social Justice, 2008

"*Rumours of a Moral Economy* is without doubt a timely book. Our society is split between the possibilities of the common good and the organization and outcomes of market economies. Now this split is acknowledged as a crucial question, and new principles of organization are proposed. Christopher Lind starts from the facts and concerns of everyday life and carries out a fascinating analysis of both the historical tendency to separate ethics from economics, as well as current debates in philosophy and sociology. Clearly, Karl Polanyi's controversial reflections on The Great Transformation couldn't but be given a central place in Lind's book."
— Michele Cangiani, Università Ca' Foscari Venezia (Ca' Foscari University of Venice)

"This book argues that there is a moral economy that exists as a coherent set of moral values embedded in strong communities. With insight and imagination, ecojustice convictions, and breathtaking historical and interdisciplinary scope, Lind elaborates in erudite and accessible prose on these values and commitments as they are revealed in times of crisis. This is a wise and stellar contribution for how to take courage together when things are not normal!"
— Dr. Marilyn Legge, Associate Professor of Christian Ethics, Emmanuel College, University of Toronto

Rumours of a Moral Economy

Rumours of a Moral Economy

Christopher Lind

Fernwood Publishing • Halifax & Winnipeg

Copyright © 2010 Christopher Lind

All rights reserved. No part of this book may be reproduced or transmitted in any form by any means without permission in writing from the publisher, except by a reviewer, who may quote brief passages in a review.

Editing: David Shulman
Cover image: *Harvesting Awareness* by Marg Janick-Grayston
Cover design: John van der Woude
Text design: Brenda Conroy
Printed and bound in Canada by Hignell Book Printing

Published in Canada by Fernwood Publishing
32 Oceanvista Lane
Black Point, Nova Scotia, B0J 1B0
and 748 Broadway Avenue, Winnipeg, Manitoba, R3G 0X3
www.fernwoodpublishing.ca

Fernwood Publishing Company Limited gratefully acknowledges the financial support of the Government of Canada through the Canada Book Fund, the Canada Council for the Arts, the Nova Scotia Department of Tourism and Culture and the Province of Manitoba, through the Book Publishing Tax Credit, for our publishing program.

Library and Archives Canada Cataloguing in Publication

Lind, Christopher, 1953-
Rumours of a moral economy / Christopher Lind.

Includes bibliographical references.
ISBN 978-1-55266-389-9 (bound).—ISBN 978-1-55266-373-8 (pbk.)

1. Economics—Moral and ethical aspects. 2. Capitalism—Moral and ethical aspects. I. Title.

HB72.L55 2010   174   C2010-902717-5

Contents

Dedicated to the memory of Professor Steve de Gruchy (1961–2010)

Acknowledgements

I want to take this opportunity to thank those who were partners in the process that led to the publication of this book. I can't name all of you but I will try to include the main categories. First of all, I want to acknowledge the Ethics and Economics students at St. Andrew's College, Saskatoon, where I first began to lay out this narrative. I especially want to acknowledge the Rev. Marg Jannick-Grayston, whose artwork graces the cover, and Rev. Roger Kett, who practically insisted that this book be published. I also want to acknowledge Dr. Gail Allan, Dr. Lynn Caldwell, Dr. Puleng Lenka-Bula and Dr. Jennifer Janzen-Ball, who continue to inspire me with their passion, commitment and good humour.

I would also like to acknowledge students at other campuses where versions of this teaching were shared. They include students in the Chalmers Summer School at VST, especially Rich Williams, who kept us all connected electronically; students in Economics and the Common Good at St. Jerome's University at the University of Waterloo, and especially Dean Myroslaw Tataryn, who made it happen; and the Moral Economy students at Emmanuel College in the Toronto School of Theology, especially Garth McNaughton, who continues to push me in a more radical direction.

Thanks go to John Cherneski, who first suggested I write a column on the moral economy so many years ago, and Barb Glen, our current editor at the *Western Producer*. Thanks as well to my co-writers of the Moral Economy Column, Rev. Rob Brown, Dr. Cam Harder, Dr. Nettie Wiebe and the readers who do us the honour of writing back and engaging with us on where a moral economy may be found.

My thanks go to researchers Holly Andruchuk, Simon Elliott and Jonathan Trentadue for their bibliographic help in the preparation of the manuscript and also to my website designer and internet guru, Brian Dench, a constant source of encouragement.

I want to express my appreciation to my editor, Wayne Antony, and all the staff at Fernwood Publishing. They are committed to the high calling of making progressive, scholarly voices heard in the marketplace, and they do a marvelous job of it.

I am in debt to the members of the Montreal-based Karl Polanyi Society, and especially Kari Polanyi-Levitt and Margie Mendell, who, with Ana Gomez, have worked tirelessly to keep space open for this kind of dialogue; also to Fred Block, Michele Cangiani and Abe Rotstein, who were generous

enough to engage in conversation about shared ideas. I also want to acknowledge the support of Massey College, its fellows and staff, and especially its
master, John Fraser, who welcomed me warmly as a senior fellow and who
enabled me to spend a year working on this book as a senior resident. I include in this group the Metcalf Innovation Fellow at Massey, Pat Thompson,
whose insight-filled conversations about vocation have helped keep my own
vocation alive.

Over the years I have been blessed by the friendship of Dr. Martin Robra
and Dr. David Hallman of the World Council of Churches, who have both
been leaders in raising up the moral dimension of economic issues especially
as it affects globalization and climate change. Life would be a lot more difficult
if it were not for my professional colleagues and friends Michael Bourgeois
and Marilyn Legge, who have encouraged me relentlessly throughout the
long birthing process.

Finally, thanks are due to my family. To my wife, Ann Elliot, for her support in the long, slow and solitary journey of writing; to my son, Aaron, for
his reminders of why it is important to articulate the boundaries of a moral
economy; and to my daughter, Emily, for her creative insight into where else
in society and culture a moral economy is emerging.

I want to dedicate this volume to the memory of Professor Steve de
Gruchy of the University of KwaZulu-Natal in South Africa. Steve was a
creative and gifted scholar, deeply committed to the principles of a moral
economy, who was just entering the full bloom of his profession when he
was taken from us at too young an age.

Christopher Lind
Toronto

Giving Life to Rumours

This book is about ethics and economics. It is also about the minimal moral standards that must be met in order for any set of economic, political and social arrangements to have legitimacy among the populations that those arrangements are meant to serve. The book is designed not to settle arguments but to start them. My hope is to stimulate conversation and reflection about what kind of economic arrangements will help create and support the world we all want to live in.

Fifteen years ago I wrote a book about the farm crisis in Saskatchewan. It was called *Something's Wrong Somewhere: Globalization, Community and the Moral Economy of the Farm Crisis*. In it I tried to interpret the crisis from the point of view of those who protested against its effects. The book used a moral economy approach, and after it was published I was approached by the editor of a new rural newspaper in Saskatchewan to write a regular column on the moral economy. There is now a team of us who write that column, and it is published in the *Western Producer*, Canada's largest farm newspaper. Many people expressed interest in the column but cannot access that paper, so I have also maintained an international email distribution list for the column.[1] So, for almost fifteen years I have been engaging the general public in Canada and globally regarding the moral dimension of economic issues.

What I have discovered in that time is that people have strong feelings and increasingly articulate opinions about ethics and the economy. This is just as true of economic issues related to the environment, health care and poverty as it is to agriculture and trade. I have yet to find an economic issue for which this does not hold true. During this time we have also endured four major collapses in the financial sector: the Asian financial crisis of 1997, the bursting of the dot.com bubble in 2000, the stock market collapse after September 11, 2001, and the most recent financial crisis of 2007–2009, the effects of which we are still experiencing as I write. Throughout this period it has become increasingly obvious that the most fundamental ethical criteria are absent from the highest level of economic decision making. In the thirteenth century, Thomas Aquinas summed up our ethical imperatives with the phrase "Do good and do no harm." This was not original to him. He was affirming what he learned from early Greek philosophers. The medical profession makes the same pledge, introduced by Hippocrates over 2,000 years ago. This simple formulation expresses a very powerful and complex moral command. How is it possible that this should be missing from Wall Street to

Bay Street, and from Whitehall to the World Trade Organization?

This book attempts to answer that question. Even more than that, however, it attempts to spell out in a public way what people say to each other behind closed doors. I have yet to meet anyone who does not want a moral economy. I frequently meet people who have already given up, and dress up their disappointment and fatigue in the self-confident cloak of "realism." To them I want to say: stop. Put your costume back in the trunk. It is right that you should want a moral economy, and furthermore such an economy is possible. The reason I say this is because we have always wanted it and have always resisted attempts to prevent or distort it. In this book you will find example after example of people creating it, reclaiming it, rebuilding it and renewing it. It is not something that can happen by itself. It only happens when people push for it and stand firmly on the boundaries of morally acceptable political and social economic arrangements and say: this far and no farther.

Building on the ancient vision of a moral economy, the emergence of moral economy as a contemporary discipline of inquiry means that there are increasing numbers of scholars willing to transcend the positive/normative divide with new analytical techniques designed to reveal the ethical dimensions of economic debate. A discussion of the issues dealt with in *Rumours of a Moral Economy* has never been more timely.

Note

1.   To read the column, or to sign up to receive it, go to www.christopherlind.ca.

1. Whatever Happened to the Ethics in Economics?

I have taught university students about ethics and economics for about twenty-five years. I tell people most of my energy goes into explaining the use of the word "and" in that last sentence. Inevitably I have students in every class who tell me they know nothing about economics. (I have yet to find a student who tells me they know nothing about ethics!) I ask them: do they have a bank account, do they have to budget their monthly income, do they pay rent or make payments on a mortgage? Invariably they engage in all or most of those activities. The obvious conclusion is they actually know quite a lot about economics, they just think they don't. I then tell them there is a reason why they think this way, and it's a political reason. There are people who benefit from this state of affairs, and it is in their interest that you believe you don't have the power to change the way things are. They speak a different language, using concepts they don't explain, and ask you to trust them to speak to the policy gods on your behalf. Economics is the new theology, and economists are the new priestly class. I guess it takes one to know one.

On the other side of the coin, many people believe that businesspeople don't have ethics. Even businesspeople believe that sometimes. Listen to the jokes we all make about business transactions.

For many of us, the more successful you are in business, the more likely

How Bailouts Work

Young Chuck in Montana bought a horse from a farmer for $100. The farmer agreed to deliver the horse the next day. The following morning he drove up and said, "Sorry son, but I have some bad news, the horse died." Chuck replied, "Well, then just give me my money back."

The farmer said, "Can't do that. I went and spent it already." Chuck said, "Okay, then, just bring me the dead horse." The farmer asked, "What ya gonna do with him?" Chuck said, "I'm going to raffle him off." The farmer said, "You can't raffle off a dead horse!"

Chuck said, "Sure I can, Watch me. I just won't tell anybody he's dead."

A month later, the farmer met up with Chuck and asked, "What happened with that dead horse?" Chuck said, "I raffled him off. I sold 500 tickets at two dollars a piece and made a profit of $998." The farmer said, "Didn't anyone complain?" Chuck said, "Just the guy who won. So I gave him his two dollars back." Chuck eventually grew up and now works for the government. He was the one who figured out how to "bail us out."

it is that you have had to confine your morality to your personal life because, after all, business is business. The price is the price and a contract is a trump card—*caveat emptor* (let the buyer beware).

My father was in the insurance business. He was with the same international company for over forty years—old school, you might say. I remember going with him one Saturday to an automobile repair shop (he expected to work at least part of every Saturday). One of his adjusters had sent a car there for repairs and he was suspicious about the quality of the work being done. Sure enough, he discovered the auto body shop was using secondhand parts but billing for new ones. He could see that the replacement door had come from a salvage yard. There were some stern words and raised voices from behind a closed door, and then we went home. When I asked what happened he replied that his suspicions had been confirmed and so he confronted the shop owner. In my most knowledgeable twelve-year-old voice I said, "I guess that's the last time you'll use that shop!" "Actually," he responded, "I will use them again. I'm pretty sure they won't do that in the future, now that they know I know. I don't want to put them out of business. We need them to stay in business but we also need them to be honest. I'm helping them do that."

My father was a businessman typical of his age. He had a strongly developed personal morality. He also had a strongly developed commercial ethic. Today we call that business ethics, but in the sixteenth century it was called "commutative ethics" because it referred to the ethics of transactions or exchange.

Ancient Attitudes Towards Commerce

That commerce is by its nature unethical is an ancient idea. The North African St. Augustine (354–430) captured the sentiment well when he wrote, "just as art cannot exist without imposture, neither can business exist without fraud" (Baldwin 1959). St. Augustine was merely continuing the biblical tradition of preferring the work of heaven to the work of this world. The Gospel of St. Matthew records Jesus teaching thus:

> Lay not up for yourselves treasures upon earth, where moth and rust doth corrupt, and where thieves break through and steal; but lay up for yourselves treasures in heaven, where neither moth nor rust doth corrupt, and where thieves do not break through nor steal. For where your treasure is, there will your heart be also. (Matthew 6:19–21)

The biblical tradition is full of instruction on fair dealing in commerce.[1]

"You shall not lend them your money at interest taken in advance." — Leviticus 25: 35–37

However, some of its most strident condemnations are reserved for "usury"—lending money at interest. Take for example the book of Leviticus, where we read the following instruction:

> Do not take interest in advance or otherwise make a profit from [your kin], but fear your God; let them live with you. You shall not lend them your money at interest taken in advance, or provide them food at a profit. (Leviticus 25:35–37)

In the book of the Prophet Ezekiel, disobedient Israelites are described as those who "take both advance interest and accrued interest, and make gain of your neighbours by extortion; you have forgotten me, says the Lord God" (Ezekiel 22:12).

These attitudes are not confined to the biblical tradition, but were present in Western culture until very recent times. In the Muslim world, prohibitions against usury are still understood by many to be prohibitions against lending money at interest. These prohibitions trace their origins to the same historical and cultural root. In the medieval period successful men of trade and commerce, at the end of their lives, would often make a moral inventory of their transgressions and attempt to make amends through their wills. Sometimes they would attempt to make restitution to those from whom they had wrested interest payments. At other times they would make charitable contributions as a kind of recompense. Codicils to their wills record entreaties for their sons not to follow their paths into trade (Heilbroner 1972: 48; Thrupp 1942: 177, quoted in Owen 2007). In the early seventeenth century we find Shakespeare putting these words into the mouth of Hamlet's future father-in-law Polonius: "Neither a borrower nor a lender be; For loan oft loses both itself and friend, And borrowing dulls the edge of husbandry" (Hamlet, Act I, Scene iii).

One of the best analyses of the transition from this long-standing attitude to money lending to the more modern approach to banking and credit is found in the English historian R.H. Tawney's *Religion and the Rise of Capitalism*. In it, Tawney describes how Christianity condemned "the unbridled indulgence of the acquisitive appetite." This was the dominant attitude until the birth of modernity in the nineteenth century and the rise of a new principle that separated commerce from religion. The Protestant Reformation was the bloody midwife, and it was Martin Luther's doctrine of two separate and distinct kingdoms, the religious and the secular, each with its own laws, which gave this development a language. It was the sixteenth-century French reformer John Calvin who gave it its method.[2] As one English cleric wrote

"Neither a borrower nor a lender be." — Hamlet, Act I, Scene iii

a generation later, "Calvin deals with usurie as the apothecarie doth with poyson" (Tawney 1937: 114). In Tawney's words:

> The claim that religion should keep its hands off business encoun-
> tered, when first formulated, a great body of antithetic doctrine,
> embodied not only in literature and teaching, but in custom and
> law. It was only gradually, and after a warfare not confined to paper,
> that it affected the transition from the status of an odious paradox
> to that of an unquestioned truth. (Tawney 1937: viii)

As we shall explore more fully in the next chapter, it was in the eighteenth and nineteenth centuries that the separation of trade from religion was transmuted into a separation of economics from ethics.[3] What is obvious here is that this change was in sharp contrast to religious tradition and only succeeded after a mighty struggle. Tawney recounts how in the Netherlands, at a time when it was the centre of European commerce and finance, a bit-ter controversy erupted over whether usurers should be admitted to holy communion and whether universities might confer degrees upon them. "It was only after a storm of pamphleteering," Tawney wrote, "in which the theological faculty of the University of Utrecht performed prodigies of zeal and ingenuity, that the States of Holland and West Friesland closed the agitation by declaring that the Church had no concern with questions of banking" (Tawney 1937: 237).

By the nineteenth century in England, the battle was over. Yet the ancient attitudes persist in the archeological layers that culture preserves. Tawney described four basic attitudes that religion may have towards social institu-tions and economic relations. The first attitude is an ascetic one: the world is fallen and the only path to holiness is one of escape. The second is one of indifference: the material world simply has no spiritual relevance. The third is one of revolution: the world may be fallen, but it can be rescued—but only through some gigantic and perhaps violent cataclysm. The fourth is one of constant reform. This attitude requires constant effort but also criticism, tolerance and adaptation (Tawney 1937: 30). All of these attitudes can still be observed in the present day.

The Rise of Economics as a Separate Discipline

Classical economists like Adam Smith argued for a market economy on moral grounds. That is, they argued that the freeing of individual initiatives within market arrangements would cumulatively operate in such a way as to serve the common good (through the mechanism of the "invisible hand"). In the late nineteenth century there was what some economists call the "marginalist revolution" in economics, through which the discipline took a decidedly more "scientific" turn, increasingly incorporating mathematical tools. The inheritors of the marginalist revolution were called "neo-classical economists."

Adam Smith thought of himself as a moral philosopher, and only much later did people start referring to him as an economist. A hundred years later Alfred Marshall taught political economy at Cambridge as part of the Moral Sciences. Although his early ambition was to become ordained, his early training was in mathematics. It was this background that helped shift the focus of his work away from relations between states ("polities"—hence political economy) and toward dimensions of purely economizing behaviour like "marginal utility." The distinction between political economy and economics still strikes some ears as a curious and unhelpful anachronism. Up until the late medieval period in Europe, discussions of commerce and economic behaviour happened within the context of discourse about justice. That means it was a part of broader discussions within moral theology and philosophy. This is why it would make sense that Adam Smith would be trained as a moral philosopher and Alfred Marshall would teach within the moral sciences. In his 1974 review of the term "political economy," Paresh Chattopadhyay traced the origin of this phrase to the early seventeenth century, noting that the modern tendency to use the unmodified word "economics" can be traced to the late nineteenth-century work of Alfred Marshall. Chattopadhyay goes on to say that while the phrase "political economy" can have several different meanings, "it is being set up [in the late twentieth century] mostly as a standard of revolt against 'orthodox' economics" (Chattopadhyay 1974: 23).

In 1890 John Neville Keynes (John Maynard's father, who was an early student of Marshall) published his *Scope and Method of Political Economy*. In that work he distinguished three types of political economy: positive science, normative science and art. While he allows for the connection of political economy with social and moral sciences, he stresses repeatedly the sharp distinction between positive economics (positive science) as the proper field of the professional economist on the one hand, and all other forms of political economy on the other. His argument was with economists trained in a historicist approach, dominant at that time in Germany. In terms of influence, the ascendancy of the neo-classical school of economics meant that

> the historical school was politely relegated to a sort of interdisciplinary no-man's land, as being more concerned with ethics and policy precepts (i.e., with the second and third concepts of political economy) than with pure, universally valid (rather than historically relative) economic science. (Deane 1978: 103)

There are two different trajectories that can be observed here. The first is the development of a discipline—from moral theology to moral philosophy to political economy to economics. The second is the development of a method—from theology to philosophy to history to mathematics. If Marshall's training in the nineteenth century was in mathematics, his explanations still used the discourse of history. By the time Paul Samuelson published his famous *Foundations of Economic Analysis* in 1947, even the explanations were in the language of mathematics, and that is what so impressed readers of the book.[4]

This latest shift within economics, from a dialogue with history to a dialogue with mathematics, came at the cost of putting ethics in the closet. The sharp distinction between "positive science" (things as they are) and "normative science" (things as they ought to be) defined questions of moral value as out of the conversation. Joan Robinson, an economist who wrote after Keynes and in his tradition, complained:

> In all this kind of analysis, the notion of ethical judgement purports to be excluded and the whole exercise is put forward as a piece of pure logic. The very idea of moral implications is abhorrent to practitioners in this field. All the same, even economists are human beings, and cannot divest themselves of human habits of thought. Their system is saturated with moral feeling. Those within it, who have grown used to breathing its balmy air, have lost the power to smell it. To those approaching from outside who complain that the scent is sickly, the insiders indignantly reply "The smell is in your own noses. Our aim is completely odourless, scientific, logical and free from value judgements." (Robinson 1963: 57)

Well into the twentieth century, history was still considered an essential part of the economist's toolkit. In the earlier years there was a prominent school of economic thought known as "institutionalism." Traditional institutionalists believe that economic behaviour is shaped by the institutions that all humans inhabit and therefore economics cannot be separated from the political and social systems in which the economy is embedded. These institutions may be formal, like political states, corporations and laws, or they may be customary, like cultures and families. Thorsten Veblen, Clarence Ayres and Harold Innis all represent this tradition, which lasted the longest among agricultural economists (John Kenneth Galbraith started out with these views). One of the last centres of institutionalist thought was found at Texas A&M University, the old Agricultural and Mechanical School, from which Clarence Ayres retired. In the 1930s there was a debate on the question of science, history and morality between Clarence Ayres and Frank Knight. Frank Knight was a friend of Ayres and a dominant force at the University of Chicago from the 1920s until the 1940s. He was also notoriously disputatious and after the third article of the exchange was published in the *International Journal of Ethics* (when was the last time two distinguished economists engaged with each other in an ethics journal?) Ayres moved quickly to claim victory:

> I have ventured the opinion that a theory of history is of crucial importance for economic theory of whatever persuasion, and that the dominant role in orthodox historical theory... was played by capital; and I am delighted to have such weighty support as professor Knight's on both these points. (Ayres 1935a: 357; see also Ayres 1935b and Knight 1935)

Since that time, some of the inheritors of the old institutionalist tradition have coalesced again around the term "new institutional economics," though with a more conservative political impact,[5] and the inheritors of Harold Innis formed themselves into a movement known as the "new political economy."[6]

The Suppression of the Ethical

It is controversial to assert that formal economic methodology suppresses ethical disagreement. The defenders of economics would argue that the positive/normative distinction properly separates ethical (normative) concern from scientific (positive) analysis.[7] The argument is not seamless, however. Even such an articulate exponent of this position as T.W. Hutchinson has acknowledged that value judgements have been suppressed, and it is extremely dangerous when that happens:

> It could be argued that through this authoritatively proposed rule regarding the separation of value-judgements about the objectives of policies, from "positive" theorizing, obtained a considerable measure of observance, it brought with it the disadvantage (as, for example with Prohibition laws) that value-judgements were not always removed or distinguished, but were driven underground or remained disguised, which could be much more dangerous and confusing than their uninhibited expression. (Hutchinson 1964: 38)

Gunnar Myrdal, the Swedish economist and Nobel Prize winner, worked in the areas of development economics and welfare economics, fields that are still concerned with normative questions. He was also critical of the positive/normative distinction because he thought it led to self-deception on the part of positivist economists. He wrote:

> By insisting on the necessity of value premises in all research, the social sciences should be opened more effectively to moral criticism. It

would then be impossible to classify economics as a "dismal science" in the sense of its being closed to moral considerations. Economists working in the conventional mode, attempting to conceal valuations basic to their research can, however, often be rightly censured in this way, and on logical grounds. (Myrdal 1969: 73)

The American economist Dierdre McCloskey has analyzed this problem from a different angle. From her point of view, the issue is not only that economists are operating on the basis of an "early 20th century understanding of certain pieces of 19th century physics" (McCloskey 1983: 484; see also McCloskey 1985), but also that economists do not actually operate on the basis of the methodology they defend. McCloskey analyzes economic arguments on the basis of their rhetoric. Following the work of the American literary critic Wayne Booth and others, she examines the metaphors and analogies economists use to explain their reasoning (Booth 1974).

Her main target here is the author of the primary textbook in most American departments of economics—Paul Samuelson—and in particular, his use of mathematics. McCloskey argues that

> the mathematics [in Samuelson's text] is presented in an offhand way, with an assumption that we all can read off partitioned matrices at a glance, inconsistent with the level of mathematics in other passages. The air of easy mathematical mastery was important to the influence of the book, by contrast with the embarrassed modesty with which most British writers at the time (Hicks most notably) pushed mathematics off into appendices. (McCloskey 1983: 500)

Hicks was following a British cultural tradition exemplified by Marshall. Mathematics is necessary, but it is not the basis of persuasion. Samuelson, by contrast, was using mathematics as a rhetorical device. Even when its use was not strictly necessary, it demonstrated his mastery of a difficult language and technique and so conveyed authority. Since Samuelson, this approach has become routine. I have personally attended public economics lectures that consisted solely of an uninterrupted series of mathematical equations. With the last equation, the argument is over. "Yet analogy and metaphor, like most of the other pieces of Samuelson's rhetoric, have no standing in the official canon" (McCloskey 1983: 501). It is no "mere rhetoric" if it is so powerful; its use becomes invisible.

Since ancient times, metaphor has been thought of as an ornament of language. Literary critics long desired to strip away the ornamentation in order to get underneath and view the plain meaning. And yet the very ideas of "stripping away," "ornamentation," "getting underneath," "revealing" and "plain" are themselves metaphorical:

The question is whether economic thought is metaphorical in some non-ornamental sense. The more obvious metaphors in economics are those used to convey novel thoughts, one sort of novelty being to compare economic with non-economic matters. "Elasticity" was once a mind-stretching fancy; "depression" was depressing; "equilibrium" compared an economy to an apple in a bowl, a settling idea; "competition" once induced thoughts of horse races; money's 'velocity' thoughts of swirling bits of paper. Much of the vocabulary of economics consists of dead metaphors taken from non-economic spheres…. Among the least bizarre of [economist Gary Becker's[8]] many metaphors, for instance, is that children are durable goods. (McCloskey 1983: 503)

McCloskey does not propose getting rid of metaphor and analogy. She just doesn't want to confuse the power of rhetorical argument with the power of thought, examination and evidence. Her target is what is sometimes known as the "Scientific Method." At other times it is known as the "Received View":

> [It] is an amalgam of logical positivism, behaviourism, operational-ism, and the hypothetico-deductive model of science…. It is best labeled simply "modernism," that is, the notion… that we know only what we cannot doubt and cannot really know what we can merely assent to.

She argues that modernism has not been carefully examined from the ground up, rather it has been accepted whole as if it were a revealed religion (McCloskey 1983: 486). "Modernism promises knowledge free from doubt, metaphysics, morals, and personal convictions; what it delivers merely renames as Scientific Method the scientist's and especially the economic scientist's metaphysics, morals, and personal convictions" (McCloskey 1983: 488). She calls the Received View arrogant because it determines worldly affairs based on epistemological convictions held independent of available evidence. For example, she argues, no study has shown convincingly that Americans were hurt by high tariffs on trade in the nineteenth century. And yet economists routinely argue that it must be true, both then and now, because that is what the theory (the Received View) says should be the case (McCloskey 1983: 493).

Economists, argues McCloskey, have uncritically absorbed the idea that concepts are stronger if they can be made measurable ("operationalism"). If they are challenged on the basis of this approach they assume their challenger is either ideologically misguided, self-interested or stupid.

"Among the precepts of modernism are:
1. Prediction (and control) is the goal of science.
2. Only the observable implications (or predictions) of a theory matter to its truth.
3. Observability entails objective, reproducible experiments.
4. If (and only if) an experimental implication of a theory proves false is the theory proved false.
5. Objectivity is to be treasured; subjective 'observation' (introspection) is not scientific knowledge.
6. Kelvin's Dictum: 'When you cannot express it in numbers, your knowledge is of a meager and unsatisfactory kind.'
7. Introspection, metaphysical belief, aesthetics, and the like may well figure in the discovery of an hypothesis but cannot figure in its justification.
8. It is the business of methodology to demarcate scientific reasoning from non-scientific, positive from normative.
9. A scientific explanation of an event brings the event under a covering law.
10. Scientists, for instance economic scientists, have nothing to say as scientists about values, whether of morality or art."
— McCloskey 1983: 484

It fits the naive fact-value split of modernism to attribute all disagreements to political differences, since facts are alleged to be, unlike values, impossible to dispute.... If one cannot reason about values, and if most of what matters is placed in the value half of the fact-value split, then it follows that one will embrace unreason when talking about things that matter. The claims of an overblown methodology of Science merely end conversation. (McCloskey 1983: 514)

The British economist, F.H. Hahn, agrees with McCloskey that "the project of a history-free understanding of the economic world is not self-evidently plausible" (Hahn 1987, 110).

The American Nobel Laureate, Robert Solo, is also keenly aware of the limited usefulness of the language of mathematics. He wrote:

Mathematics is the appropriate instrument of prediction, but economics and the social sciences cannot be refuted through experimental prediction. And where credibility must be established through a judgement based on the direct observation of function and practice, mathematics is the worst of all possible languages. (Solow 2001: 355)

Solo also suspects that the real function of mathematics in economics is to serve as a secret language monopolized by a technical elite, effectively shielding economics from outside observation and critical evaluation (ibid.).

Max Weber argued that one of the problems with capitalism in the twentieth century was that it eroded the moral foundations that it had required for its earlier success. It encouraged acquisitiveness and undermined both honesty and frugality (savings) (Weber 1976). R.H. Tawney was very much of the same view (Tawney 1920). To use a contemporary example, as first-hand accounts emerge of the collapse of the U.S. secondary (or "subprime") mortgage market, it is becoming apparent that the people who sold this debt to investors knew it was a highly risky investment. They didn't care about the risk because once they sold it to a new buyer it was no longer their own problem. Their greed undermined their commitment to honesty. The development economist Albert Hirschman convincingly demonstrated that Weber's thesis merely revived for a new generation an argument made throughout the eighteenth century by John Wesley and Adam Smith, and in the nineteenth century by Karl Marx. It would also be made by others later in the twentieth century, for example Joseph Schumpeter, Herbert Marcuse and Daniel Bell (Hirschman 1982: 1468).

Of course, Hirschman himself stands in a long line of thinkers arguing the opposite position—namely that market society performs a character-building function. David Hume held this position in the eighteenth century, and T.H. Green was its advocate in the nineteenth (Hansen 1977: 94). Hirschman's claim that, as a matter of historical fact, wealth is not diverted from savings into conspicuous consumption is a harder argument to make in 2010 than it was in 1982, after we have seen so much wealth diverted into homes, yachts and gold bathroom fixtures.

This debate about rhetoric, metaphor, method and discipline cannot be reduced to a debate about the politics of the left and the politics of the right. Indeed, it is a curious phenomenon that economists of left and right should be equally suspicious of the concern for values, though for different reasons. For economists in the mainstream of capitalist society, those operating under the spell of the Received View, values are impediments to rational judgement. For political economists in the Marxist tradition, values are necessary ideological commitments. For the latter group, a politically neutral standpoint is not only undesirable but impossible, and therefore claims of such neutrality are fraudulent. However, the ideological dimension looms so large for this group that all value claims are thought to revolve around the question of ideological preference. Therefore, when an ethical point is made it is thought to be an unnecessary intrusion into the debate about the moral superiority of socialism. Within their own ideological framework, Marxist political economists are just as unwilling to grant space to an ethical debate. Like their capitalist colleagues, Marxist political economists have a tendency to assume the legitimacy of their ends in such a way that all discussion about means is reduced to a discussion of technique.[9]

Western culture has a history of suspicion of commerce and trade. The activities are thought of as impure at least in part because they encourage the cultivation of impure (immoral) motives. Nowhere was this theme more fully developed than in discussions of usury. Economizing behaviour was well known and praised, but commercial transactions were thought of as a subset of justice, making all economics a subset of morality.

The language of political economy emerged in the sixteenth century as people began to examine wealth creation in terms of the actions of political states. The violent civil and religious struggles of this same period included the attempt to protect private property from interference by the church and then from interference by the state. The moneylenders of 500 years ago are but the precursors of today's merchant and investment banks, like Goldman Sachs and Lehman Brothers. The Heavenly Princes and the Earthly Princes needed their services in equal measure. The papacy needed money to defend itself against the Protestant Reformation. German states needed money to fund the Thirty Years' War. Spain and Portugal needed to invest in their naval fleets to consolidate their colonial expansion in Latin America. However, the borrowers could as easily begin popular campaigns against the lenders, based on religion or ethnicity, and end up confiscating their assets. The bankers and the merchants needed protection and worked hard to overcome that dependence. By the eighteenth century this campaign for independence achieved the separation of business from government.

Subsequently, the nineteenth-century campaign against poverty, and for wealth, succeeded in separating economics from politics. Since politics is just another way of describing social ethics in practice, it was this same campaign that separated ethics from economics. The separation was a formal one, intended not to eliminate moral concern but rather to better serve it. The split seemed permanent when the discipline of economics took on that of mathematics as its formal dialogue partner in place of the discipline of history. However, because the separation is morally grounded, arguments for and against it are placed squarely within the field of moral discourse.

If you want to find the ethical dimension of conventional economic discourse, strip away the metaphors and get underneath the rhetoric. What will you find there? Why, more metaphors and rhetoric of course—not because that is wrong but because that is real. Remain skeptical of the discipline's overblown methodological claims, and if an economist offers up a prediction as if it has been revealed, ask if you can stick your fingers in his or her side.[10]

Back to My Father

My father did not have a strongly developed social ethic, and he would have agreed with the proposition that ethics and economics do not mix because economics is governed by its own laws. However, his personal morality was clear and his ethical approach to business did sometimes cause his gaze to lift to the horizon. He was ninety-one when he died. During his fifty years in business, he tried to teach me some lessons about life and money. This is what I learned:

When you make an agreement, write it down.

I came from a family of five children. Every Saturday, allowance would be dispensed like cups of navy grog—five cents for the youngest, twenty-five cents for the oldest and gradations in between. These dispensations were recorded in a ledger with deductions for misbehaviour. Disputes about who received what were resolved by reference to the ledger. As we grew older, allowance stopped and loans began. Each transaction was private, but each was accompanied by a promissory note. When you make an agreement, write it down.

Cut your cloth according to your needs.

As an orphan, my father could not afford to go into debt. He bought only what he needed and what he could afford. He didn't drive when he could cycle and he didn't cycle when he could walk. He was always well dressed, but if you looked closely you could see that his clothes were always well mended. It was from him that I learned how to darn socks. He had learned the difference between wants and needs. "Don't cut your cloth according to your wants," he would say, "cut it according to your needs."

Don't forget where you come from.

My father befriended a man who lived alone in a rooming house in a neighbouring city. What little family this man had, he was alienated from. My father picked him up hitchhiking and brought him by our house where he was paid to do some gardening. We called him Popeye because he spent most of the time on the verandah, smoking a borrowed pipe and telling stories about the war. This went on for years. One day, after we had driven him home, I asked my father why we did this. He said, "There was a time when I had no family to speak of and I lived in a boarding house too. Don't forget where you come from, that could be you."

Pick up the pennies and the dollars will take care of themselves.

My father was an inveterate recycler. He saved newspapers and rolled them into fireplace logs. He never discarded anything if he could avoid it. He took special pleasure in his early morning raids on the local lovers' lane where he could collect bottles and cans to be returned for cash. It was inconceivable to him that one would pass by a penny on the street and not pick it up. "Pick up the pennies," was his motto, "and the dollars will take care of themselves."

Every budget, no matter how small, has room for the common good.

Every week my father attended church and made his financial contribution. This was in addition to other charities he supported regularly. We received our allowance on Saturday, but on Sunday we were expected to donate a portion to the church. These days we are all encouraged by our governments, if not our culture, to set up a registered retirement or savings plan and pay ourselves first. This was not my father's view. His view was that first of all we need each other in order to survive. Therefore, investment in community is a necessary expense, and every budget, no matter how small, has room for the common good.

Notes

1. "A just weight and balance are the Lord's: all the weights of the bag are his work." Proverbs 16:23.
2. See also the German sociologist Max Weber's seminal work *The Protestant Ethic and the Spirit of Capitalism*, first published in English in 1958. Weber and Tawney disagreed in important respects about the relationship of the Protestant Reformation to the rise of a capitalist economy. Weber thought Protestantism was determinative while Tawney thought the Protestant movement was merely permissive of capitalist development.
3. "The new economy entailed a de-moralizing of the theory of trade and consumption no less far-reaching than the more widely debated dissolution of restrictions upon usury" (Thompson 1971: 89).
4. "[It] drastically redirected the advanced study of economics toward greater and more productive use of mathematics" (Cooper 1997).
5. See for example the International Society for New Institutional Economics.
6. There are many schools of thought and disciplinary conversations that use this handy moniker. See for example Shah and McIvor 2006. In this case, I am thinking of a specific Canadian conversation best represented by Daniel Drache and Wallace Clement 1985.
7. Andrew Sayer describes the positive/normative distinction this way: "In positive thought, we assume that if our ideas fail to fit the world, we should change them to fit the world. By contrast, in normative thought, when we perceive a mismatch between our thinking and how the world seems to be, we assume that

the world needs to be changed to fit our ideas" (Sayer 2005: 215).

8. Gary Becker is an American economist, Nobel Laureate and professor at the University of Chicago. He is famous for applying the tools of economic analysis to topics typically studied by sociologists.

9. See my analysis of how Canada's Catholic bishops made use of dependency theory (Lind 1983).

10. This is a Christian reference to the disciple Thomas, who didn't believe that Jesus had risen from the dead until he stuck his hand in the wound on Jesus' side (John 20:25).

2. Remembering a Moral Economy

Did you forget where you put your keys last night? Do you sometimes forget the name of your best friend? Forgetfulness is common, especially as we get older. But some things are important to remember and others we want to forget. When we have painful or traumatic experiences we seem to approach them in two common ways. One voice says we should forget them in order to put them behind us—get on with our lives. Another voice counsels us to remember the pain because if we submerge it beneath the surface of our conscious mind our lives will be directed by hidden forces and we will never be truly free.

In South Africa, the Truth and Reconciliation Commission created the conditions for the facts of life under apartheid to be told. By validating the truth of ordinary people's experience, the Commission made sure that what they had been through could never be denied. South Africans would always have to remember who they had been and where they came from.

Soon it will be August 6 again. In 2010 it was sixty-five years since we (the "Western allied powers" of World War II, including Canada) dropped the first atomic bomb on Hiroshima, and three days later a second one on Nagasaki. Over 200,000 people died as a result of those two bombs. We remember those events, but for what purpose, to what effect? Remembering the atomic bomb means remembering our capacity to do the most unspeakable things to each other. In order to be free we have to remember what horrors we are capable of. We remember so that it will never happen again. We cannot truly commit to change our behaviour unless we confess what our past behaviour has been. We want to remember ourselves as compassionate, caring and just. We want to think of ourselves as good. We can act justly in the future if we make a point of remembering with clarity our prior willingness to do the opposite.

Across Canada every December 6, there are memorials to the fourteen young women who were gunned down at Montreal's École Polytechnique in 1989. They were all engineering students and their crime was being female. Their names are Anne-Marie Edward, Anne-Marie Lemay, Annie St. Arneault, Annie Turcotte, Barbara Daigneault, Barbara Maria Klucznik, Genevieve Bergeron, Helene Colgan, Maryse LeClaire, Maryse Leganiere, Maud Haviernier, Michele Richard, Nathalie Croteau and Sonia Pelletier.

Canadians remember this event because it is important to remind ourselves that society is still so patriarchal that being female can get you killed.

We will never be free of this hatred if we allow ourselves to forget. So, we remember with a purpose.

What else must we remember, and for what purpose? How about a moral economy? This term has been reintroduced into contemporary scholarship by the British historian E.P. Thompson. He is most well known for his book *The Making of the English Working Class* (1964) but more relevant for our purposes are two articles. The first one, "The Moral Economy of the English Crowd," was published in 1971. The second, "Moral Economy Reviewed," was published in the 1991 collection of his articles entitled *Customs in Common*.

Thompson (1924–1993) was a historian of eighteenth-century England. In the 1961 article Thompson was arguing against those historians who interpreted the actions of rioting eighteenth-century crowds as nothing more than spasmodic responses to hunger. In Thompson's view, these crowds were engaging in well-planned actions (not spasmodic) that represented a kind of civil disobedience against innovations in commercial practice. They were defending traditional rights and customs. They were remembering a different way of doing things and the broad public support they enjoyed reflected an older moral consensus among the working poor. Thompson writes:

> It is possible to detect in almost every eighteenth century crowd action some legitimising notion. By the notion of legitimation I mean that the men and women in the crowd were informed by the belief that they were defending traditional rights or customs; and, in general, that they were supported by the wider consensus of the community. On occasion this popular consensus was endorsed by some measure of licence afforded by the authorities. More commonly, the consensus was so strong that it overrode motives of fear or deference. (Thompson 1991: 188)

These traditional rights and customs had to do with what were considered legitimate and illegitimate practices when it came to markets, milling, baking, price setting and the proper economic roles of different members of the community. All of these taken together constitute what Thompson calls "the moral economy of the poor" (ibid.).

Two stories from 1795 might illustrate why some historians described events as a spontaneous riot and why Thompson interpreted them differently. In the village of Handborough, Oxfordshire, a wagon carrying sacks of flour and wheat was stopped. A number of women climbed aboard and threw some of the sacks down to the ground, while others declared they would pay 40 shillings per sack or they would have it for free. "The owner (a 'yeoman') at length agreed: 'If that must be the price, it must be the price.'"

In the same year, the baker Thomas Smith, carrying loaves of bread on his horse, was accosted by forty women on the streets of Hadstock, Essex.

Several women demanded that he sell the bread to them at 9 pence per quarter-gallon loaf while he held out for 19 pence. When several women began removing the bread without payment, he quickly agreed to their price.

If this were an example of a spontaneous riot we might expect all the flour, all the wheat and all the bread to be taken without recompense. If so we might call it theft, if not looting. Instead, what is remarkable is that this action is preamble to a kind of bargaining. What the women were insisting on was a "just price" in a time of famine, and they were remembering what a just price was:

> What is extraordinary about this pattern is that it reproduces, sometimes with great precision, the emergency measures in times of scarcity whose operation, in the years between 1580 and 1630, were codified in the Book of Orders. These emergency measures were employed in times of scarcity in the last years of Elizabeth, and put into effect, in a somewhat revised form, in the reign of Charles I, in 1630. (Thompson 1991: 224)

Thompson's moral economy of the poor was based on the older paternalist model of provision in the context of a subsistence economy. In that feudal model, the local lord or landowner or village squire had formal responsibility to care for the peasants and serfs in his villages. It is this set of social and economic arrangements that was under attack by the newly established free market, supported by the ideology of "laissez-faire" and articulated by the new political economists. The hitherto normal assumption was that food grown in a region should be consumed in that same region, except with regard to surpluses, which could be exported. In times of scarcity it was the duty of those in power to ensure that the poor were able to provide for themselves.

So, all food to be sold was required to be brought to market on market day. When the first bell rang, it was the peasant and local farmer who were first allowed to shop for small quantities. What the women were later rebelling against was the novel practice of selling grain before harvest while it was still standing in the field, or a landlord bringing to market only samples of his crop as representative of what he had for sale. The people knew these practices were illegal and appealed to local magistrates to enforce the law, only to find that the magistrates were loathe to side against the lords, on whom their own livelihood also depended. So, the crowds decided to enforce the laws themselves. They were not reckless, but disciplined. They were not stealing, but rather "setting the price" according to ancient convention. Of course, the moral economy also broke decisively with the paternalistic model because its popular ethic sanctioned direct action by the crowd, whereas the values of order underpinning the earlier model obviously did not.

The crowds were not as violent as was alleged by some of the wealthy, but the threat of violence seems to have had a sobering effect. In 1812 in Nottingham, "the women paraded with a loaf upon a pole, streaked with red and tied with black crepe, emblematic of 'bleeding famine decked in Sackecloth'" (Thompson 1991: 234). Violence was on display, but so too was restraint. In 1766 the sheriff of Gloucestershire wrote that the mobs had committed many acts of violence that year, "some of wantonness and excess; and in other instances some acts of courage, prudence, justice, and a consistency towards that which they profess to obtain" (Thompson 1991: 258).

It is hard not to notice how often women seemed to be at the forefront of these confrontations. Partly this is because women did most of the face-to-face marketing and would be the first to realize if they were being cheated or refused. There are cases on record of potato dealers in Pembroke being pelted by women using the merchants' own produce. It was also partly because they had made the calculation that they enjoyed slightly greater immunity from the authorities. There are other reports of women in Northampton, equipped with knives, going to market to force down the price of grain, supported by men who would intervene only if the women were molested; and a magistrate in Haverfordwest suggested that women were confident in their actions because they knew the soldiers "were for them and would do them no hurt" (Thompson 1991: 233). In some cases where the women were ineffective or lacked sufficient courage, there are reports that entire mines would suddenly halt work as all the tin miners and colliery workers (300 strong in one case) headed to town to set the price of grain. The women remembered the law and insisted that it be enforced. Justice in commercial relationships and care for the community were key elements of their identity. By remembering the law and acting on this memory, they refused to allow the diminishing of their values and insisted that those values be carried forward into the future.

There were numerous specific grievances that set off the riots. They ranged from soaring prices caused by "forestalling" (buying produce before it comes to market), "regrating" (buying and reselling at a higher price within the same market) and "engrossing" (holding back produce while waiting for the price to rise), to other malpractice by merchants and grain dealers such as shorting the weight or adulterating the flour. Sometimes they were even sparked by raw hunger. However, when common people protested, they appealed to a common consensus regarding legitimate and illegitimate practices in the food trades. They were remembering a time when these moral standards were not in dispute. "An outrage to these moral assumptions, quite as much as actual deprivation," writes Thompson, "was the usual occasion for direct action" (1991: 188).

The powerful emotions brought on by the exploitation of life-threatening emergencies gave a particularly "moral" charge to the protests. On the other hand, according to Thompson, in peasant and early industrial communities, we find many so-called "economic" relations governed by non-monetary norms. They exist as "a tissue of customs and usages until they are threatened by monetary rationalizations and are made self-conscious as a 'moral economy.' In this sense, the moral economy is summoned into being in resistance to the economy of the 'free market'" (Thompson 1991: 340).

The term "moral economy" might seem modern but it actually has an ancient pedigree. The American philosopher Ralph Barton Perry published a book by this title in 1909; however, the book has nothing to do with modern economics or even the moral economy in Thompson's sense. Rather, it is a book about the internal and logical structure of morality in the same way that theologians talk about the economy of God as the internal and logical structure of the Godhead (Perry 1909). Thompson thought the term in his sense dated back to the late eighteenth century. Thompson (1991: 337) quotes the political reformer Bronterre O'Brien (a Chartist), who used it in 1837 in a polemic against political economists:

> True political economy is like true domestic economy; it does not consist solely in slaving and saving; there is a moral economy as well... it is indeed the Moral Economy that they always keep out of sight. When they talk about the tendency of large masses of capital, and the division of labour, to increase production and cheapen commodities, they do not tell us of the inferior human being which a single and fixed occupation must necessarily produce.

In the thirteenth century, Thomas Aquinas described commercial transactions as falling under the category of "commutative" justice (what constitutes a fair price) as opposed to "distributive" justice (what constitutes a fair share) and "retributive" justice (what constitutes a fair punishment). His argument is based on customary usage and some commentators see such strong parallels between what Aquinas was describing in the thirteenth century and what Thompson wrote about the eighteenth century that they feel justified in writing about the "moral economy of Aquinas."

All of these are subsets of justice. Prior to the birth of modern economic thought all behaviour, including economic behaviour, was seen to fall under

"The resemblances [between the just price arguments of Aquinas and the moral economy of Thompson's crowds] are striking. They are so striking, in fact, that one might be inclined to term the "moral economy" of the crowd and the moral obligations found in Aquinas (through duty and mutual advantage in action) as little short of synonymous notions." — Owen 2007: 17

the judgement of moralizing authorities like the monarch, the church and the conscience of the individual.

Thompson argues that the moral economy of the poor is summoned into being as a response to the attack on customary rights in the practice and ideology of the free market. What is the new reality that emerged at the end of the eighteenth century? Adam Smith tried to systematically explain its logic when he wrote *The Wealth of Nations* in 1776. However, for our purposes the best interpreter of the phenomenon is Karl Polanyi.

Karl Polanyi and Market Society

Karl Polanyi (1886–1964) was a Hungarian-born intellectual. Trained as a lawyer, he had brief careers in politics (as secretary of the national bourgeois Radical Party) and the military (as a cavalry officer in the Austro-Hungarian army in World War I)[1] before becoming a refugee in Vienna in 1919 and again before and during World War II. He worked as an editorial writer for the German-language equivalent of the *Economist* magazine (the *Österreichische Volkswirt*), and was hired to teach economic history by the Workers Educational Association (WEA) in England. From 1940 to 1943 Polanyi taught at Bennington College in Vermont, where he completed work on his most famous book, published in 1944 under the publisher's title, *The Great Transformation*.[2]

After World War II he lived in Canada and commuted to Columbia University in New York where he again taught economic history, this time with a significant impact on anthropology. His wife, Ilona Duczynska, was denied a U.S. visa because she had been a member of the Hungarian Communist Party before World War I, even though she was expelled from the party in 1922 (Vezér 1990) for being too much of a free thinker.

Polanyi's overwhelming desire was to understand and explain the new age in which he was living. He begins his great work with an observation presented as fact: "Nineteenth century civilization has collapsed." His own challenge was to come to terms with "the political and economic origins of this event, as well as the great transformation which it ushered in" (Polanyi 1944: 3).

Polanyi understood nineteenth-century civilization to rest on four institutions which had now collapsed: The balance-of-power system in international politics, the liberal state, the international gold standard and the self-regulating market. Writing in the middle of the second of two world wars, it is not surprising that he should think both that the balance of power had fallen apart and that the liberal state had been supplanted by dictatorships of both the right and left. He lived long enough to see another balance of power emerge in the Cold War, but not long enough to see the Soviet Union—the "Empire of the East"—implode under pressure from the Empire of the

"Democracy for us is not a system of rule, but the ideal way of life. We shall never accept the dictatorship of the proletariat, just as we have rejected the dictatorship of the ruling classes." — Karl Polanyi (quoted by György Litván in Kari Polanyi-Levitt 1990)

West (1989–1991). He saw the liberal state re-emerge as the welfare state, but did not survive to see it captured by the neo-liberal state. He lived to see the gold standard re-established, but not to see it abandoned by President Nixon in 1971 because it hindered American military ambitions. As for the self-regulating market, he considered it obsolete and ready to be replaced. Indeed, he thought the future of human society demanded it (Polanyi 1947). So, he may have been off in his timing, but he was not wrong in describing the general trajectory of his time.

All four institutions are important and Polanyi deals with each of them in detail. However, the key to the whole system in the nineteenth century lay "in the laws governing market economy." He called it the "fount and matrix of the system" (Polanyi 1944: 3).

Obviously Polanyi is describing the rise of capitalist economy, but he uses the term "capitalism" rarely. According to Fred Block, this is both a deliberate effort to distinguish his work from that of Marx and also evidence of a development in his thinking. The triumphalist defenders of capitalism assume that all economies organized around the pursuit of profit in a market context have a common essence and therefore will produce similar institutional arrangements. (In an eerie echo of Marx, some even argue that democracy is a necessary result of free markets.[3]) By using the terms "market economy" and "market society," Polanyi allows for the development of different varieties of capitalism; instead of focusing our attention on the modes of production when addressing the shift from feudalism to capitalism, as Marx would, Polanyi makes us look at the social relations transformed by that same shift (Block & Polanyi 2003: 299). Polanyi had read Marx and was influenced by Marxism throughout his life. However, he rejected those determinist versions of Marxism that limited free will, just as he rejected the idea of the dictatorship of the proletariat. Polanyi was a socialist for whom Marxism provided a frame of reference and a proponent of the guild socialism associated with John Ruskin, Robert Owen and G.D.H. Cole.[4]

Polanyi's Thesis

Polanyi's thesis in *The Great Transformation* is that prior to the Industrial Revolution in Great Britain, economic relations were submerged in social relations. Markets existed, currency was exchanged and economic activity was engaged in, but the economy, understood as a sphere of action separate from society, did not exist. The economy was embedded in society, much as it always had been. Economic activity was regulated by politics and by custom so that economic goals were understood to be subordinate to political and social goals. With the rise of the machine age, symbolized by the steam engine, productive activity started to shift from agriculture to manufacturing and from the countryside to urban areas. Markets played a larger and larger role in society with prices increasingly set by the play of supply and demand rather than by regulation. The new wealth created in this way became disconnected from the existing system of social protection which assumed feudal arrangements.

When markets became linked they formed a market system, and it was this formation that caused the relationship between economy and society to be reversed. Economic relationships became disembedded from society and formed their own space called "the economy." When this happened the economy began regulating society rather than the other way around. Society began to be refashioned to meet economic goals instead of the reverse. The political philosophy that endorsed this development was known as "laissez-faire"—meaning it advocated letting markets operate free of regulation.

Polanyi considered this political project to be disastrous, impossible and indeed utopian. At the beginning of his treatise he wrote:

> Our thesis is that the idea of a self-adjusting market implied a stark utopia. Such an institution could not exist for any length of time without annihilating the human and natural substance of society; it would have physically destroyed man [sic] and transformed his surroundings into a wilderness. Inevitably, society took measures to protect itself, but whatever measures it took impaired the self-regulation of the market, disorganized industrial life, and thus endangered society in yet another way. It was this dilemma which forced the development of the market system into a definite groove and finally disrupted the social organization based upon it. (Polanyi 1944: 3)

The market economy began to dissolve the older social structure. These were the changes noted by E.P. Thompson. When food prices in times of famine were set by the fluctuations of supply and demand, the poor were no longer protected. This meant the bonds of mutual obligation, of reciprocity, typical of the older feudal society became fatally weakened. This revolutionary idea, that social relations should be determined by economic forces, acted not just to reshape some social relationships but rather as a universal solvent to dissolve them all. There was no part of society left untouched. The market economy had become disembedded and therefore dangerous to social welfare. This produced in turn the need to re-embed the economy: the Great Transformation.

"The title *The Great Transformation* refers, of course, not to the breakdown that resulted, but to the reconstitution of an institutional structure that would restore the primacy of social organism over social mechanism and embed once more man's economy within the norms and values of his social existence." — Abraham Rotstein, "The Reality of Society: Karl Polanyi's Philosophical Perspective," in Polanyi-Levitt 1990:100.

Fictitious Commodities

In order for markets to successfully link up and form a market system, Polanyi identified three other changes that had to happen. Three fundamental aspects of social life also had to be (re-)organized according to the principles of a self-regulating market. These were humanity, nature and capital (otherwise called labour, land and money). Market relationships govern the trading of commodities. What is significant about labour, land and money is that they are either not produced for sale, as in the case of people, or they are not produced at all, as with land. They are fictitious commodities. However, when they are forced into market relationships we no longer talk about human communities but we are rather obliged to talk about the supply and demand for labour, with the price described as wages. We no longer talk about "creation" or nature, for which we have some responsibility, but rather of the supply and demand for minerals, forest products and agricultural commodities which we can produce or consume, buy, sell or lease.

The effect of these changes was that market economy produced market society. In this society there were only two motives governing human behaviour. These were hunger and gain "or, more precisely, fear of going without the necessities of life, and expectation of profit" (Polanyi 1947: 111).

Political advocates of the free-market philosophy, the laissez-faire liberals, argued that supply and demand should be allowed to set a proper price in the markets for these proto-commodities. Throughout the nineteenth century, when these policies were followed, massive famines were allowed to wreak their havoc (Ireland 1845–1852 and India 1876–1878), and wholesale migrations occurred as people sought to save themselves from privation and indifference. This is why the resurgence of this philosophy in the late twentieth century has been called a "neo-liberal" movement, even though many of its exponents call themselves "conservatives."

The fundamental contradiction of this period is that the reality of a "self-regulating" market—free markets for labour, land and money—has to be created and maintained by the active intervention of political agents. The state has to intervene in order to prevent self-preservation initiatives. As Bruce Berman notes, at the same time as market liberals were using the power of the state to force labour, land and money into self-regulating markets, they were also justifying their efforts on the basis of the market as a feature of nature governed by scientific laws (Berman 2007: 8).

Today, as we experience another revolution (called "economic globalization") we are faced with the same contradictions. Some essential features of our common life, like capital flows, are deregulated, while others, like labour, cannot be liberalized without opening up national borders to massive migration. The effects of the resulting tensions are enormously painful. As Fred Block puts it:

> Nations that offend the sensibilities of traders in the financial markets can find themselves subject to huge capital outflows and intense speculative pressures against their currencies. Once again, these arrangements are justified by their consistency with the principle of market self-regulation. However, within societies, governments—even in the most market-oriented polities—continue to play a central role in economic life by organizing the key fictitious commodities (land, labor, and money) and by engaging in a wide variety of protective measures. Hence, the same deep tensions between an international monetary system based on principles of market self-regulation and national policies based on quite different practices characterize our own historical period. (Block & Polanyi 2003: 288)

Polanyi's logic is that when you completely expose labour, land and money to the principles of self-regulation you end up destroying society itself. That is why even market societies have to find some way of re-embedding the economy in social relations. This concept of embeddedness distinguishes Polanyi both from advocates of liberal capitalism and from advocates of Marxist socialism, since both groups believe that social institutions are determined by the economic system, and not the other way around (Polanyi 1947: 110).

Speenhamland

According to Polanyi, the last of the fictitious commodity markets to be created was the market for labour. The Poor Law of 1601 had made the administration of the poor rates the responsibility of each parish, but the rate of relief was not uniform and some people were thought to have moved parishes in order to take advantage of more generous provisions. The Settlement Act of 1662 effectively tied labour to its parish by requiring that labourers have a settlement certificate if they were to move. This certificate was a promise by their original parish to continue providing poor relief if necessary. Since parishes were reluctant to provide such assurance, labourers tended to stay put.

In 1793 Britain again became involved in wars in France. Food became more difficult to import from Europe and there were shortages caused by a series of poor harvests. As the price of bread started to rise, local authorities began to fear civil unrest. On May 6, 1795, the Magistrates of Berkshire met at the Pelican Inn in the District of Speenhamland (near the village of Speen) and decided that subsidies to the poor should be linked to the price of bread, bringing them up to a subsistence level. For example, where a gallon loaf of second-quality bread costs 1 shilling, then a single man should receive, from wages or subsidy, 3 shillings per week and a family of four should receive 7 shillings and 6 pence. Where a gallon loaf cost 1 shilling and 6 pence, the minimum income should be 4 shillings and thruppence for a single man and 10 shillings and thruppence for a family of four.

This system became known as the "Speenhamland System." While not codified as legislation enacted by Parliament, it became a widespread practice and was relied upon as an emergency measure until its abolition in 1834 with the passing of the Poor Law Amendment Act. This act eliminated what was known as "outdoor relief" and reduced the options available to the able-bodied poor to a choice between starvation and the workhouse. The workhouses were deliberately made to be mean, petty and cruel. Families were broken up, children forced to work and clothes exchanged for a woolen cloth with the letter "P" (for "pauper") sewn on.

There has been a great deal of new scholarship on this period of English history since 1944 because there are three powerful but conflicting narratives that have emerged out of it. The first narrative is that this kind of poor relief interferes with the natural functioning of the market mechanism. A subsidy disconnected from employment encourages unemployment and also encourages overpopulation. This narrative, popular with the Poor Law Commissioners who met in 1832, reflects the attitude of Thomas Malthus, who published his *Essay on the Principle of Population* in 1798, and also of Joseph Townsend. In his *Dissertation on the Poor Law of 1786*, Townsend recounted a parable of a Pacific Island populated by dogs and goats, the island of Robinson Crusoe. Townsend argued that just as the populations of goats and dogs reached an equilibrium as they each adjusted to the changing food supply, so would the population of human poor naturally reach equilibrium were it not for the artificial intervention of poor relief.

Polanyi's analysis of Townsend needs no further elaboration. Polanyi wrote: "Hobbes had argued the need for a despot because men were like beasts; Townsend insisted that they were actually beasts and that, precisely for that reason, only a minimum of government was required" (Polanyi 1944: 114).

The second narrative is that while the Berkshire justices attempted to put a floor under wages, they actually erected a ceiling. Since the parish would provide a supplement regardless of the wage rate, wages would tend

"Hunger will tame the fiercest animals, it will teach decency and civility, obedience and subjection, to the most perverse. In general it is only hunger which can spur and goad them [the poor] on to labour; yet our laws have said they shall never hunger." — Joseph Townsend (quoted by Polanyi 1944: 113)

to decline since the parish, rather than the employer, was responsible for the difference between wages paid and what was required for subsistence. This narrative was also popular with the Poor Law Commission of 1832 and has been repeated for generations, right up to the present day. It was used to argue against a Family Assistance Plan proposed by President Nixon in 1969, and against a guaranteed annual income plan proposed by Canadian Prime Minister Chretien in 2000 (Block and Somers 2003: 284).

The third narrative was that the Speenhamland system reinforced the power of the older landowning feudal classes against the emerging capitalist class. The Speenhamland system encouraged labour to stay in rural areas whereas capitalists needed labour in the cities. It lowered costs for landlords, increased costs for urban capitalists and lowered productivity all around. This analysis was accepted by Marx and Engels and, in an adapted form, by Polanyi.

For Polanyi, the most devastating impact of Speenhamland was not narrowly economic but more broadly social and cultural. He calls the transition's impact from self-support to welfare support a process of "pauperization"— "But for the protracted effects of the allowance system," Polanyi writes, "it would be impossible to explain the human and social degradation of early capitalism" (Polanyi 1944: 80). For Polanyi (1944: 101), these effects made it necessary to overcome this pauperization:

> The abolishment of Speenhamland was the true birthday of the modern working class, whose immediate self-interest destined them to become the protectors of society against the intrinsic dangers of a machine civilization. But whatever the future had in store for them, working class and market economy appeared in history together.

The newer research on the Poor Laws indicates that there are some problems with the details of Polanyi's analysis of Speenhamland. The practices reflected in the legislation of 1601 actually date back to the late thirteenth century. There was much more variation in Poor Law practices than Polanyi acknowledges, as parishes experimented with a variety of measures to protect the poor and maintain incentives to work. Payments did rise sharply at the end of the eighteenth century but this was largely restricted to the wheat growing and pastoral areas of southeastern England, where cottage industries were in decline.

Furthermore, the conventional narrative treats wage-price indexing as a Speenhamland innovation, when it was clearly used in the fourteenth century (the 1349–51 Ordinance and Statute of Labourers) and the sixteenth century (the 1563 Tudor Statute of Artificers). Bread scales were also used at other times of high bread prices in the eighteenth century. Also, the rise in relief payments in the late 1820s cannot be understood apart from the unemployment created by the introduction of the threshing machine and the famous Captain Swing riots, which followed in 1830.

Where Speenhamland was in effect, it did succeed in protecting the poor from the ravages of low or absent wages but it had just as powerful an effect as an allegory. The Royal Commission of 1832 argued that productivity was reduced by the system, but we now know that there is evidence that contradicts that claim. Instead we see that the logic of the Commissioners was already present in the stories told by Thomas Malthus and Joseph Townsend. According to Townsend, hunger and starvation is nature's way of bringing the population of goats and dogs into equilibrium on an island, and Britain is an island after all. According to Malthus, if you remove the restraint of hunger by feeding the poor in a time of famine, you only contribute to overpopulation and increase the competition for scarce food.

It was this allegorical environment in which the modern discipline of economics was born. The nineteenth century saw the formation of the last market for fictitious commodities (labour), the linking of markets to form a system of markets and the resultant birth of market society. The stark characterization of human behaviour as being governed by only two motives, hunger and gain (fear of starvation and the profit motive), was true at this time because it was made to be true. The social solidarity of the old order was abandoned in favour of a scientific approach that was thought to be as reliable as the principles governing the steam engine.

E.P. Thompson has given us a broader context in which to interpret this social upheaval. It wasn't just Speenhamland but the whole Industrial Revolution that pushed the old order off its mount. Between 1818 and 1826 relief rates fell by 25 percent and national income was rising steadily. Even

"Falling prices and limited credit forced farmers to reduce labor costs [producing]... chronic rural unemployment and increased use of poor relief.... Low wheat prices forced the more successful farmers to put increasing resources into labor-saving technology such as the threshing machine. Since hand threshing of wheat could represent as much as one-quarter of the whole year's quantity of farm work, mechanization had a huge impact on the rural demand for labor in the winter months. Triggered by these high rates of unemployment, the machine smashing in the Captain Swing riots of 1830 exploded. This outbreak of rural disorder played a key role in undermining elite support for the Old Poor Law." — Block and Somers 2003: 310

during the 1830s relief rates continued to fall. Without economic chaos, why should there be social chaos? To understand, we need to return to Polanyi's conviction that the worst devastation was cultural, not strictly economic. Polanyi (1944: 157) writes:

> A social calamity is primarily a cultural not an economic phenomenon that can be measured by income figures or population statistics.... Not economic exploitation, as often assumed, but the disintegration of the cultural environment of the victim is then the cause of the degradation. The economic process may, naturally, supply the vehicle of the destruction, and almost invariably economic inferiority will make the weaker yield, but the immediate cause of his [sic] undoing is not for that reason economic; it lies in the lethal injury to the institutions in which his social existence is embodied. The result is loss of self-respect and standards, whether the unit is a people or a class, whether the process springs from so-called 'culture conflict' or from a change in the position of a class within the confines of a society.

Double Movement

Market economy was born through the midwifery of economic liberalism, which advocated a doctrine of laissez-faire. Since Polanyi's argument is that market economy poses a threat to the "human and natural components of the social fabric," (1944: 150) we should expect to find in the historical record spontaneous and varied attempts to protect that same social fabric. Polanyi offers just such evidence. He cites lists (1944: 146) of all kinds of legislation passed by liberals and anti-liberals, in England and elsewhere throughout Europe, at various times during the second half of the nineteenth century. He includes factory laws, social insurance, municipal trading, health services, public utilities, tariffs, bounties and subsidies, cartels and trusts, embargoes on immigration, on capital movements, on imports, in his lists of spontaneous acts of protection (1944: 144). His point is that market economy refashioned society, but since market society is inherently unstable, since its inception we have experienced the uninterrupted need to re-embed economic relations within social relations. Polanyi describes this as a "double movement" and this concept, along with the concept of the "embedded economy," is another unique contribution he makes to modern political and economic analysis. First there is a process causing economic forces to become disembedded from the control of social relations; in a second step, this becomes so dangerous to social well-being that society takes measures to protect itself.

Polanyi describes the forces of change and Thompson adds details of the historical record. However, it is important to be clear that this first step of disembedding the economy is in no way "natural" or inevitable. Rather, the removal of restraint, giving free rein to these new forces and commercial and technological innovations, was a political act and entirely intentional. The dismantling of the old Poor Law was an act of Parliament. It was justified by a political ideology of laissez-faire that was utopian in character. The utopian ideology was not only endorsed with the power of a new science, the science of society, but was also justified with a new moral language, the ethics of utility. In utilitarian ethics there is no common good separate from a collection of individual goods. The net benefit of goods and bads can be calculated with a kind of arithmetic. The goods and bads are evaluated not on the basis of motives, intentions or duties but rather on the basis of consequences.

Under the influence of this utopian ideology, society is forced to break relations of solidarity and begins to refashion itself in ways that make sense economically. The second step of this phenomenon is observed regardless of leaders' political persuasion. A disembedded economy is so dangerous that political parties of both the left and the right seek ways to control it. We see this vividly today, after the economic crisis of 2008–9, when parties otherwise wholly committed to capitalism use public resources to nationalize banks, set executive pay levels and seek to increase support for homeowners and the unemployed. In the early nineteenth century David Ricardo was the most popular economist advocating laissez-faire ideology. Ricardo was channeling the spirit of Townsend in seeking an equilibrium between supply and demand in the market—between goats and dogs on the island. In the late twentieth century, the most popular economist advocating the ideology of free trade was Milton Friedman—renewing the theological anthropology of rugged individualism (now known as neoliberalism) where only an unencumbered market system could balance the theoretically infinite number of choices between starvation and private profit.

The second half of the double movement is not inevitable, though in the end it may be irresistible. It was delayed in England from the 1830s until the 1870s. Today we can see that it has occurred in several waves. The crisis of the Great Depression in the 1930s led to the reforms of the New Deal and then the creation of the welfare state in the 1950s and 1960s. The foreign exchange markets were disembedded after 1971 when the U.S. abandoned the gold standard, as were the financial markets when an unregulated global market in financial capital was created on a new scale. We called this process economic globalization. Markets for fictitious commodities were created by the political agents of the nation-state. Money is traded on the basis of contracts and these contracts are enforced by legal (state) regulation. It is hard to imagine how the market economy would function if government really did stay out of it!

It is this disembedded financial economy that has now shown itself to be

"Polanyi lays the basis for understanding that tax policies, technology policies, competition policies, and trade policies are not incidentals, but fundamental to structuring how different market societies operate." — Block & Polanyi 2003: 300

so dangerous that the whole world is scrambling to find ways to re-regulate it—to re-embed it in global society.

Under globalization, the market for money was no longer regulated by society, unlike the market for labour. The imbalance in wealth creation that resulted, whereby the rich get richer and the poor poorer on both a national and a global level, has been the main force behind the "unprecedented movement of peoples towards the developed capitalist metropoles [from postcolonial societies] as both political and economic refugees" (Berman 2007: 16).

Even in China we see the same phenomenon. As Beverly Silver and Giovanni Arrighi have written:

> China's movement toward integration into the global "self-regulating market" has been accompanied by a strong countermovement for the self-protection of society. The main protagonists of this countermovement are workers who have been laid off from state owned enterprises, as China's quest for global economic competitiveness has gone hand in hand with massive layoffs and the dismantling of China's welfare state (the smashing of the "iron rice bowl"). (Silver & Arrighi 2003: 349 n89)

Through Polanyi's concept of the embedded economy we can now see why technological and commercial innovations are sometimes championed by advocates of market liberalism in order to reduce or eliminate the restraints imposed by law or custom, and how those changes are sometimes resisted by protesters relying on older moral and customary expectations. We can also see the devastating consequences of complete market freedom and how populations across the political spectrum unite to create the new regulations required to protect society. Market society is constantly reshaped by this movement between the two poles of embeddedness and disembeddedness. As Fred Block (Block & Polanyi 2003: 296) put it:

> [T]he critical point is that... [as] Polanyi elaborates the multiple forms of protection, he discovers the concept of the always embedded economy—that market societies must construct elaborate rules and institutional structures to limit the individual pursuit of gain or risk degenerating into a Hobbesian war of all against all. In order to have the benefits of increased efficiency that are supposed to flow

from market competition, these societies must first limit the pursuit of gain by assuring that not everything is for sale to the highest bidder. They must also act to channel the energies of those economic actors motivated largely by gain into a narrow range of legitimate activities. In summary, the economy has to be embedded in law, politics, and morality.

Formal versus Substantive Economics

In later work Polanyi pushed at the theoretical implications of his earlier historical analysis. If our assumption about all societies being market societies was wrong, how then can we understand economics? He concluded that we needed a new toolbox which treated the economy as a "social process," thereby widening the scope of our investigation. He said that humans may be capable of "economizing action" but that "there is no necessary relationship between economizing action and the empirical economy":

> The institutional structure of the economy need not compel, as with the market system, economizing actions. The implications of such an insight for all the social sciences which must deal with the economy could hardly be more far-reaching. Nothing less than a fundamentally different starting point for the analysis of the human economy as a social process is required. (Polanyi et al. 1957: 240)

He called what he was trying to do "institutional analysis." His fundamentally different starting point had to do with distinguishing between the study of market phenomena (which he called formal economics) and the study of "the whole range of man's [sic] material want satisfaction" (which he called substantive economics) (Polanyi 1957: 241). The formal meaning of "economic," he wrote,

> derives from the logical character of the means-ends relationship, as apparent in such words as "economical" or "economizing." It refers to a definite situation of choice, namely, that between the different uses of means induced by an insufficiency of those means. If we call the rules governing choice of means the logic of rational action, then we may denote this variant of logic, with an improvised term as formal economics.

This is what we would call today mainstream economics. The substantive meaning of "economic"

> derives from man's dependence for his living upon nature and his fellows. It refers to the interchange with his natural and social en-

vironment, in so far as this results in supplying him with the means of material want satisfaction. (Polanyi 1957: 243)

Polanyi acknowledges that his conceptual use of the substantive economy is unfashionable (1957: 240) and even that all earlier attempts to achieve a naturalistic economics were unsuccessful. This was so, he argued, because no naturalistic economics can compete "with economic analysis in explaining the mechanics of livelihood under a market system" (Polanyi 1957: 240–1). His concern, though, is to relativize formal economics. It is a useful form of inquiry but only one of many disciplines that concern themselves with the economy. Should it become normative it may positively hinder the work of the anthropologist, the sociologist and the economic historian. It is also on this basis that his distinction proves useful for the ethicist.

The formal meaning of "economic" implies rules governing choices made between different uses of scarce means. Formal economic analysis can prove effective within the limitations of a market system, but only within that system. Formal and substantive terms will coincide, Polanyi wrote, where the empirical economy (the reference point for a substantive approach) is controlled by a system of price-making markets (the reference point for a formal approach) (Polanyi 1957: 244).

> In the whole range of economic disciplines, the point of common interest is set by the process through which material want satisfaction is provided. Locating this process and examining its operation can only be achieved by shifting the emphasis from a type of rational action to the configuration of goods and person movements which actually make up the economy. (Polanyi 1957: 241)

The substantive definition implies neither choice nor scarce means. From this perspective the economy "is an instituted process" (Polanyi 1957: 248). It is a process because it involves materials changing places or changing hands (locational movements and appropriative movements). It is instituted because it is characterized by institutions which perform specific social functions and possess specific histories. When the economic process becomes instituted, it acquires

> unity and stability; it produces a structure with a definite function in society; it shifts the place of the process in society, thus adding significance to its history; *it centres interest on values, motives and policy.* Unity and stability, structure and function, history and policy spell out operationally the content of our assertion that the human economy is an instituted process. (Polanyi 1957: 250)

Because the human economy is an instituted process, it is a process which is embedded in both economic and noneconomic institutions.

> The inclusion of the noneconomic is vital. For religion or govern-
> ment may be as important for the structure and functioning of
> the economy as monetary institutions or the availability of tools
> and machines themselves that lighten the toil of labour. (Polanyi
> 1957: 250)

This is what Polanyi means when he says that the market economy is
historically exceptional because it has institutionalized the motive of "gain"
as the principal reason for material interaction. People have acted in history
in a material fashion, for religious and other reasons. In a market society it
is increasingly thought to be "irrational" to act materially for reasons other
than personal profit.

In summary, the formal view grew out of the specific social conditions of
the eighteenth century, in which that analysis did correspond approximately
to the empirical reality. It continues to define mainstream North American
economics today. Since the middle of the nineteenth century, however, society
has attempted to re-embed the economic process in order to ensure its own
continued existence. We continue to be hampered, though, by the intellectual baggage of that period, namely Adam Smith's view of innate human
behaviour as trucking, bartering and exchanging. Polanyi has attempted to
supersede the market as our frame of reference. By using a substantive approach, he has attempted to develop "a wider frame of reference to which
the market itself is referable" (Polanyi 1957: 270).

From an ethical point of view, Polanyi's identification and development
of a substantive approach to economic relationships makes a difference in
at least three ways. In the first case, since formal economics enshrines the
assumptions of the utilitarian ethic, it subordinates all other social values to
that of efficiency, as defined by the market system (that is, as the economizing
of self-interested behaviour). The substantive approach renews the possibility
and the hope of different social and economic arrangements, according to
different moral values and visions.

Secondly, the substantive approach provides some new tools that will be
needed if we will actually identify and transform specific moral economies.
It should be noted in this regard that the term "substantive" has tended not
to be used by other economists—even those directly influenced by Polanyi.
I am thinking here of David Ross and Peter Usher who contrast the formal
with the informal economy, and also of Abraham Rotstein who has done
the same.[5]

The third way the substantive/formal distinction is helpful has to do with
the status of discourse about ethics, and ethical discourse, among practising
economists. Polanyi's description of the substantive approach as concerning
itself with the "interplay of humanity with the social and natural environ-

ment" could as well be a description of the heart of social ethics. By contrast, formal economics suppresses ethical disagreement by treating as extraneous the utilitarian ethical assumptions on which the formal approach is based. This leaves neither the social space nor the conceptual nor linguistic tools to engage with real moral differences.

Reality of Society

The political poster child for neoliberalism in the late twentieth century was the British Prime Minister Margaret Thatcher. In 1987, in an interview with the magazine *Women's Own*, she famously said, "Who is society? There is no such thing."

This quotation proves an irresistible backdrop to another theme that follows from Polanyi's historical analysis, one which I would describe as methodological. Polanyi argued that the market system destroyed society as it was then known. In the process of its destruction, society was discovered. That is, society came to be seen as something that was not simply achieved (bringing civilization out of chaos, for instance), but as something that could be created in one way or another. Society was discovered to be something malleable, a human construct. In the case of economics, the formal market economy remade society in its own image, hence, market society.

Polanyi relativized formal economics and cautioned against it becoming normative lest it hinder the legitimate work of the anthropologist, the sociologist and the economic historian (Polanyi 1944: 241). Polanyi was able to relativize formal economics by engaging in the methodological shift of starting with the reality of society instead of the reality of the formal economy. This methodological shift is an important one for anyone who considers themselves to be a social critic. Polanyi showed that the market economy was historically exceptional in the sense of being unique.

So first of all, we can see that so-called noneconomic factors and alternative motives may be crucial in the operation of any empirical economy. Secondly, the methodological starting point of society rather than market economy allows for the inclusion of variables and data not normally part of the economist's trade. When the Canadian Catholic Bishops intervened

"I think we have gone through a period when too many children and people have been given to understand "I have a problem, it is the Government's job to cope with it!" or "I have a problem, I will go and get a grant to cope with it!" "I am homeless, the Government must house me!" and so they are casting their problems on society and who is society? There is no such thing! There are individual men and women and there are families and no government can do anything except through people and people look to themselves first." — Margaret Thatcher, Interview with *Women's Own*, Oct. 31, 1987

in a national economic debate in January of 1983, their starting point was their pastoral experience and moral concern. It is precisely this attention to family violence, addiction and the human degradation of unemployment that can become a legitimate and significant starting point when we choose to begin by looking at society instead of the market. It is also where most of civil society engages with the debate.

There is a third implication of the reality of society. Abraham Rotstein elaborated this theme in a philosophical direction. He described Polanyi's "reality of society" as an elliptical, subtle and complex metaphysical doctrine. He suggests that it would be a misunderstanding "to think of it simply in an institutional or sociological context" (Rotstein 1986: 17).

Rotstein understands Polanyi to have revised his earlier understanding of the reality of community as the relationship of persons. From Rotstein's (1986:14) point of view, the reality of society means that the moral freedom of the individual has been fundamentally compromised in a way that we cannot avoid but we may be able to transcend:

> Power and economic value together are the moral Achilles heel, so to speak, of the complex society. They point to an alien and external realm of social existence which has been spawned by the unavoidable wishes and choices of the members of the community. We cannot turn our faces away from the moral consequences of these spheres of activity since these networks are our collective progeny. As they run loose, they may fatefully compromise others. Yet we cannot disown them for we are the constituents of that complex society.

While Rotstein uncritically affirms Polanyi's tendency toward hyperbole by suggesting that the knowledge of society fits within a Hegelian framework of the transformation of human consciousness—analogous to the knowledge of death and freedom (for Hegel a knowledge of human liberty required a conscious awareness of death and human limitation)—I agree that we must take into account the knowledge of the reality of society. I think it is actually happening in contemporary religious ethical discourse, and from my own field I can give two examples. One response to the feminist critique of ethics is to develop an understanding of the moral life in terms of relationships in community, rather than in terms of the accountability of power (i.e., caring rather than justice) (Heyward 1982; Welch 2000). Carol Gilligan's critique of the moral development theory of Lawrence Kohlberg, on the basis that he studied only boys and not boys and girls, is a secular example of this de-

For Polanyi there are three revelations that are formative in shaping Western consciousness: "knowledge of death, knowledge of freedom, and knowledge of society."
— Rotstein 1986: 15

velopment. Gilligan noted that when boys played a game in the schoolyard they argued about the rules of the game so much that arguing seemed like it was part of the game. By contrast, when girls played they would argue and then stop the game lest relationships among the group were harmed (Gilligan 1982).

A second example involves the emergence of solidarity as an appropriate understanding of practical religious ethics. This is not just a solidarity of worker with worker based on self-interest, but a solidarity with the poor by the non-poor and other popular-sector groups for the sake of peace and justice, otherwise known as the common good. This is a significant shift away from the older understanding of Christian mission as the conversion of the individual to a new pattern of belief. Though not articulated as such, the move within Christian circles away from individual categories based on assumptions of freedom and power, toward relational, communal and social categories, does reflect, I think, the knowledge of the reality of society. This knowledge is experienced as a limitation on the viability of categories of being and doing in isolation from the being and doing of others. It reflects the third lesson to be drawn from Polanyi's methodological category of the reality of society as starting point, and the essence of what Rotstein describes as Polanyi's metaphysical doctrine.

That third lesson is the reality of society as limitation and opportunity. It is no longer possible to think of the individual as the primary moral category whose characteristics are normative for society. Modern industrial society is now so complex and interdependent that if one had to take individual responsibility for all the moral considerations involved in every economic transaction, no one would get out of bed in the morning. Rotstein is right to suggest that there is no longer an inviolate moral space to which the individual can retreat.

The other side of the ledger is that if we can reclaim the relational side of our being, as persons-in-community, we can ensure the freedom from social calamity that is necessary if freedom for individual expression is to be available to all. I have already pointed to signs of this transformation in feminist moral criticism and the contemporary Christian left. The next level of engagement will be in struggles to institutionalize the solidarity required for true mutuality.

The final implication of this chapter's analysis is the recognition that all economies are embedded in social structures. There is no actually existing place called "the economy" governed by a logic and rationality all its own, as market liberals and some Marxists believe. People who advocate this line of thinking are trying to persuade us that all our public policy choices must be limited by the need for consistency with market rationality.

On the contrary, all social structures have a moral character. So, we can say that all economies are moral economies. All economies are regulated by political processes or made possible by legal structures enforced by the state. Those processes and structures reflect a moral consensus among those with political power. We may consider that consensus illegitimate for any number of reasons (such as dictatorship, or maldistribution of power through class, gender or racial prejudice, for example), but that doesn't mean there isn't a moral character to the economic arrangements. It only means any particular economy might be considered immoral. This is probably the most important reason why so much argument on economic matters takes the form of a debate about justice.

Notes

1. For biographical details of Karl Polanyi see Lee Congdon, "The Sovereignty of Society: Polanyi in Vienna," in Kari Polanyi-Levitt (ed.), *The Life and Work of Karl Polanyi*, Montreal: Black Rose Books, 1990; and Linda McQuaig, *All You Can Eat*, Toronto: Penguin 2001, esp. chapter 4, "Love and Revolution in Red Vienna."

2. The title Polanyi proposed for his book was *The Political and Economic Origins of Our Time*. This was used by the publisher as a subtitle. Page numbers for quotations are taken from the 1957 edition published by Boston's Beacon Press.

3. Marx thought that socialism could only arise through the development of capitalism's contradictions. That is, once capitalism had produced enough material goods for everyone's satisfaction and the conflicting interests of the owners of capital and the workers (the proletariat) had developed sufficiently, then a revolution would overthrow the ruling classes and socialism would result. See Marx & Engels 1959: 43–44.

4. See also Ferenc Músci, "The Start of Karl Polanyi's Career," and Lee Congdon, "The Sovereignty of Society: Polanyi in Vienna," in Kari Polanyi-Levitt 1990.

5. See David Ross and Peter Usher, *From the Roots Up: Economic Development as if Community Mattered* (1986); and Abraham Rotstein, *Rebuilding from Within: Remedies for Canada's Ailing Economy* (1984).

3. Community as a Basis of Resistance

There are at least two ways to extend Thompson's analysis of the moral economy. It can be extended in time, from the eighteenth century to the modern day, and across space, from Anglo-Saxon culture to other cultures around the world. In both these ways, the idea can be expanded conceptually. In particular, I will analyze the moral economy in terms of four principles: sufficiency, sustainability, equity and solidarity. These four principles don't represent the core of the moral economy. Rather, they represent the boundaries of tolerance. If elites try to press their class or power advantage beyond these boundaries, the people will consider direct action to be both necessary and justified. They then engage in a disruption of social peace to restore moral order to society.

Three stories will illustrate these analytical extensions. The first is the story of Scottish crofters from the Outer Hebrides, manipulated into Canadian emigration in the nineteenth century. The second is the story of a small village in Malaysia coping with the impact of the green revolution in agriculture. And third is the story of immigrant cleaners organizing to achieve a living wage in London in the twenty-first century.

The Saltcoats Crofters

In western Canada, in the middle of the broad sweep of prairie where bison used to thunder by for days at a time, stands a small town named Saltcoats. It is named after a scenic town with sandy beaches on the west coast of Scotland where they used to distil sea salt in tiny waterfront "cots." These days it is probably best known as the place where Paul McCartney was vacationing when he composed his elusive song "Mull of Kintyre."

The town (pop. 494), in the province of Saskatchewan, was named after the Scottish village because it was the home port of the Allen Steamship Line, which brought Scottish immigrants to Canada. But this pleasant bit of geographic trivia hides a much darker story about how the Scots were dispossessed at home and in turn became inheritors of land dispossessed from the indigenous people of the prairies.

In the 1860s, in what was then known as the Northwest Territories of Canada, a campaign against the bison herds gradually led to their disappearance and almost to their extinction. They were a primary food source for the indigenous peoples, and their destruction led to widespread starvation. Eventually, the hunger became one of the primary causes of the Northwest

Rebellion of 1885, led by the Metis leader Louis Riel. The first treaties with the Crown were signed in this region in the 1870s, and this continued through the 1880s. Lack of food was one of the reasons treaties were accepted by the indigenous peoples, along with the spread of new diseases like smallpox. The treaties made land available for a transcontinental railroad as well as for settlement by Europeans.

In the 1880s, life was also desperate for the poor inhabitants of the Scottish highlands and the western islands. For the previous hundred years or more, the common grazing lands, where the poor had customary rights to graze their few livestock, had gone through a process of enclosure as landlords sought a stronger base for a sheep grazing economy. The enclosure of the commons led to widespread starvation and also to rebellion. The rich came to see the poor as a problem, and made efforts to clear the troublemakers from the area. The strategy thought most likely to succeed was a plan to encourage emigration to the colonies.

In the Outer Hebrides, on the islands of Lewis, Harris, North and South Uist, Benbecula and Barra, the enclosures were compounded by other disasters. Only twenty years earlier they had faced hunger as a result of the same potato blight that caused the Irish famine. Now they faced a crisis in the fishery. In 1882 the crofters[1] at Braes on the Isle of Skye went on a rent strike against forced evictions. The constabulary called in from Glasgow were confronted by women and children armed with sticks and stones. The political impact of this resistance was enormous. It encouraged other crofters, and rent strikes and invasions of deer forests became so widespread that this episode became known as the "Crofters' War" (Norton 1994: 2). It led to a Commission of Inquiry and various political reforms, including the Crofters Act of 1886 (see Devine 1994).

By 1887, the focus of highland discontent had shifted to Lewis, the largest of the Outer Hebridean islands. It was the only part of the highlands that had not experienced a decrease in population since the 1850s. According to the census of 1886, its population amounted to 27,000 souls. The crisis in the fishery was caused by a dramatic decline in the price of herring due to record catches and an increase in the import duties imposed by European governments (Devine 1994: 235). This caused the crofter and cottar groups on the island to demand increased agricultural land. The urgency of the demand was underlined by a raid in November of 1887 on the Park Forest and the slaughtering of enough deer to feed the hungry. The largest landowner on the island was Lady Matheson. A generation earlier, 44,000 acres had been enclosed to make a sheep farm. The enclosure meant the dissolution of many townships and the displacement of many crofters. When the lease for the sheep farm came up for renewal she was approached by many crofters who wanted to rent small parcels once again, but she refused. It was then converted into a deer park for wealthy sport hunters from the mainland (see Macleod 1987).

After the experience of the Battle of the Braes, the government knew that police would be ineffective and so sent a detachment of Royal Scots Guards followed by a deployment of Royal Marines. Although the instigators of the raid were arrested (and later acquitted):

> Several delegations of crofters and cottars met with Lady Matheson, the island's major landowner, urging her to redistribute the land. It was to one of these delegations that she uttered her famous statement: "These lands are mine and you have nothing to do with them." (Norton 1994: 10)

Lady Matheson then left the island for Paris, eventually retiring to the south of France, where she died in 1896.

Malcolm McNeil was a Hebridean (Barra) and a native Gaelic speaker. A retired army officer, he was an inspector with the Edinburgh Board of Supervision for the Relief of the Poor. He was also a staunch advocate for emigration as a solution to the Highland "problems." In January of 1888, McNeill wrote to Lord Lothian (Secretary for Scotland) that

> the bulk of the population of Lochs [on the Isle of Lewis] and elsewhere will be brought face to face with the necessity of killing their cattle and sheep to sustain life, while those who have no stock must either appeal to the parochial board or starve. (Norton 1994: 10)

McNeill was successful in persuading the government to sponsor an emigration scheme. He recommended the Canadian Northwest because a provision in Canada's Dominion Lands Act allowed for the enforcement of an obligation to repay a government loan. The original plan was for the resettlement of as many as 30,000 families and he recommended that "emigrants sail directly to Canada from their home parishes to avoid 'socialistic' influences at Glasgow and Greenock" (Norton 1994: 7). However, he wanted it done quickly.

On the May 5, 1888, McNeill arrived in Stornoway on the Island of Lewis and asked the island's church ministers to announce to their congregations that he would meet prospective emigrants on Monday, May 7. At that meeting he announced, "In exchange for a promise to repay a loan of £120, each family head was to receive title to a grant of 160 acres of farmland in Canada" (Norton 1994: xv). The only complication was that they had to be prepared to leave from Stornoway in one week's time, on May 14, in order to set sail from Glasgow on May 19. As it happened, prospective emigrants had between four and seven days to arrange affairs. A similar announcement was made on the Isle of Harris but they had no more time than the Lewis group had—namely, seven days at best. This was a dark choice for the Hebrideans. Leaving the islands probably meant leaving for good, never to return. Furthermore, leaving also meant relinquishing their ancient claims to the land from which they felt they had been unjustly dispossessed. Finally, in a cash-poor economy, neighbours and relatives did not possess the money with which to purchase the holdings being left behind, so emigrants were not able to realize anywhere near the amount of cash they hoped for to seed their new life. Some needed an advance on the promised loan, just to clear their debts with local merchants.

The first group was destined for settlement near Killarney, Manitoba. A year later the process was repeated, and on April 3, 1889, a second group left, destined for Wolseley in present-day Saskatchewan (over 200 miles west of Killarney).[2] The main difference this time was that no monetary advances would be made to pay Scottish debts. So, the second group had even fewer resources than the first. Thirty-three family heads declared no cash resources at all, and only three families declared assets over £10.

McNeill's plan to have the crofters leave directly to Canada from their home parishes was not possible in this initial phase. There was a three-day layover in Glasgow and while arrangements were made for families to stay in the "sailors' home" owned by the Allan Line, they were met in Glasgow by Gaelic speaking members of the local police force and guarded for the duration by officers in plain clothes (Norton 1994: 17). The fear seemed to be less that they would be influenced by socialists than that they would be persuaded by members of the Highland Land Law Reform Association not to abandon Scotland. Indeed, members of the Land League were awaiting them at the docks.

The journey to Canada was a long one, and, unbeknownst to the settlers, negotiations had not been finalized with the Canadian government. In the end, with regard to the second group of settlers, the Imperial Colonization Board returned to earlier discussions with the railway, which also had land available for settlement. "Less than twenty-four hours from Winnipeg, the new immigrants were told that their destination was no longer Wolseley, but rather Saltcoats, at the terminus of the Manitoba and North Western Railway, in Assiniboia [present day Saskatchewan]," almost a hundred miles away.

The story is ultimately one of optimism tempered by enormous obstacles and hardship. Two days after arrival, one of the islanders was married at the Saltcoats railway station to her fiancé, who had arrived with the 1888 settlement group at Pelican Lake near Killarney. One adult and two children died from illness shortly after, and the medical treatment of others was hindered by their inability to pay for doctors' fees and medication. The railway officials had decided upon homestead locations regardless of settler preferences. Some thought the railway wanted to disperse the islanders in order to prevent political action.

> Each family head was conveyed to the site chosen for him approximately ten miles north of Saltcoats; forty-six initially refused to accept the selections. [Railway Agent] MacNutt later stated that the parish groups wanted to settle together, and the eventual settlement pattern did reflect Scottish parish origins. Fourteen families insisted on locations of a more purely prairie character than those the company was offering. That group settled in an adjacent township on land the company had not intended to offer. As much as a month was taken up by the process of site selection....
>
> Some of the men, under the impression that houses were to be built *for* them and not *by* them, refused to unload and haul their own lumber unless paid to do so. To avoid further delay they were paid ten cents an hour. The amounts were later charged against their advances.... Two distinct colonies had been formed. Fourteen families... became known as the King Colony; thirty-three families... became known as the Lothian Colony. (Norton 1994: 39)

The story of the Saltcoats colonies four years on is equally disheartening. Originally there had been forty-nine families. Two of the families had refused the land offered and joined relatives at Moosemin and Killarney. Of the remaining forty-seven, at least half had abandoned the attempt to secure title to a quarter section of land (160 acres) and moved on. Appeals for emergency clothing for the settlement were heard during that time at least twice in Presbyterian churches in Winnipeg.

The experience of the Scottish colonizers was so far from what they had been promised that the plan to entice 30,000 families was abandoned. Even so, when the Imperial Colonization Board issued its final report in 1906, it boasted that "all moneys advanced had been recovered due to land sales and repayments from the emigrant crofters and their descendants" (Norton 1994: 89).

When we think about the Lothian emigration scheme and the Saltcoats settlers in particular from the perspective of E.P. Thompson and the moral economy of the English crowd, the parallels are obvious. A profound economic change was exploited by the most powerful. The poor, by which I mean the majority of people, found their traditional rights and customs were no longer supported by the elites and insufficiently backed up by the law and government institutions. They remembered an earlier time when their needs were respected and protected, and they engaged in direct action by raiding the deer forest and demanding their rights. From there the stories diverge, of course. However, if we consider the stories in a more thematic and systematic way, we can see some clear principles to which the people are responding. I am going to call these "the principles of a moral economy." They represent the boundaries of tolerance. Within these moral boundaries, the people will tolerate a great variety of economic arrangements even though they may grumble and complain about changes. However, when these boundaries are crossed, the moral offence is considered so egregious that a violation of social order is warranted. These principles can be organized around the themes of sufficiency, sustainability, equity and solidarity.

Sufficiency

What drove the crofters to direct action was poverty and the threat of starvation. There wasn't enough to eat. The enclosure of their common grazing lands meant that they had become even more dependent on the sea for food and wages. In the earlier part of the nineteenth century, many on the west coast of Scotland earned cash wages by gathering kelp and burning it to make soda ash, used in the manufacture of soap. However, the rise of free-trade sympathies in the government led to the removal of tariffs on soda ash and the consequent collapse of prices. This left fishing as the one remaining industry available, and when fish prices collapsed in the 1880s, there were no local options easily available. With the collapse of the local cash economy, the subsistence economy was all that was left. The refusal of the largest landowner to open up the deer park for more crofts meant there was insufficient food to supply the growing population. From the point of view of the crofters, not only were their customary rights being violated by Lady Matheson but it was also morally wrong for twelve square miles of land to be set aside for a blood sport instead of ensuring sufficient food for the needy. "They viewed deer forests as a sin against mankind, and blood sports as a brutal lust, and they were sworn to abolish deer forests and blood sports" (MacLeod 1888: 1).

In addition, sufficiency was also an issue once the islanders arrived in Saltcoats. There was extensive discussion about the minimum resources required for subsistence. McNeill attempted to recruit smaller families, and families with older children, so there would be more labour available for the hard work of breaking the land. There were debates about whether a loan of £120 would be enough and several requests for additional funds were made to government.

"Another petition was sent on the 3rd January 1883, humbly praying [Lady Matheson] to remove the deer and give her starving cottars an opportunity of mere subsistence, but it, too, received the same treatment—deer was of much more account than the starving families of Lochs." — Macleod 1888: 5.

Sustainability

The crofters' economic condition was exacerbated by the collapse of fish prices, notably herring. We now know that overfishing of herring in the North Sea is a problem of environmental sustainability. When McNeill wrote to Lord Lothian that "the bulk of the population of Lochs [on the Isle of Lewis] and elsewhere will be brought face to face with the necessity of killing their cattle and sheep to sustain life," he was saying that the conditions at that time were unsustainable and the next development would be crofters killing their milking cows or breeding livestock in order to prevent starvation. This is roughly equivalent to a starving farmer eating the seed corn to survive the winter, though it means having no seed to plant in the spring. When the first boatload of immigrant crofters arrived in Canada too late to plant seed for that year's harvest, they were faced with exactly that dilemma—eating the seed corn to survive and not having any seed to sow when the land was finally cleared and ready for planting.

Equity

The moral principle of equity is in part a claim about fairness. The crofters had many grievances that took the shape of complaints regarding fairness. It wasn't fair that the cottars had been dispossessed by the clearances of the last century. It wasn't fair that Lady Matheson had enclosed the common grazing lands and removed several townships to make way for more sheep. When the lease for the sheep farm was due to expire, it wasn't fair that she refused to lease some of the land for additional crofts. It wasn't fair that the desires of rich hunters engaging in a blood sport should take precedence over the needs of the hungry crofting families. It wasn't fair that the preachers announced the meeting with McNeill about emigration instead of announcing meetings of the Land Law Reform Association. It wasn't fair that fundamental decisions affecting the livelihood of a whole community could be made by a single landlord, instead of by the people affected.

These grievances persisted in the new country. It wasn't fair that decisions about the allocation of homesteads were made without consultation with the heads of families. It also wasn't fair that the first round of emigrants received advances on their loans before they left, but the second group did not.

Solidarity

This moral principle is also much in evidence throughout this story. The Land League was campaigning against the Lothian emigration scheme because it was violating the tenets of solidarity. The emigrants were accused of "abandoning Scotland" and weakening the fight for justice in land rights. The complaint against Lady Matheson was not only about her lack of compassion or charity. It was also a complaint about the elites' lack of solidarity with the poor. Elites were maximizing their economic advantage by enclosing land for sheep or hunting, leaving the deprived and dispossessed to starve or leave. The deer raiders were expressing solidarity with their landless neighbours through their direct action. They weren't just killing the deer to eat (some of them got sick from too much rich meat). They were trying to eliminate the deer so it would be economically attractive to rent out the land as crofts once more.

In the New World, solidarity emerged as an important principle once again. The Saltcoats settlers wanted to homestead according to their parish pattern and not be so distant from one another. Even the administrators recognized that if they could settle newcomers near to existing settlements there would be increased support and therefore a higher likelihood of successful adaptation. Indeed, in Killarney, there was a larger existing settlement that was able to do exactly that by renting potato land and hiring wage labour.

The Moral Economy of the Peasant

E.P. Thompson seems to have coined the term "moral economy" in opposition to the idea of the market economy, which he also thought of as a "metaphor (or mask) for capitalist process" (Thompson 1991: 305), even though he believed he was borrowing the term from the late eighteenth century. In his original essay he described it as "a consistent traditional view of social norms and obligations, of the proper economic functions of several parties within the community, which, taken together, can be said to constitute the moral economy of the poor" (Thompson 1971: 188). In the end, he acknowledged that the term had outgrown his own limited use of it. Two years before he died he wrote, "If I did father the term 'moral economy' upon current academic discourse, the term has long forgotten its paternity. I will not disown it, but it has come of age and I am no longer answerable for its actions" (Thompson 1991: 351). As a historian, Thompson was careful to keep his analysis rooted in very specific communities, histories and records lest the analysis "bleed off the edge into uncontextual moralistic rhetoric" (Thompson 1991: 341). His supporters and disciples, however, have been keen to extend the analysis, and one of the most prominent and most successful has been the American political scientist James C. Scott.

The preceding story of the Saltcoats crofters extended the moral economy analysis forward by a century, but Scott stretches the analysis in two ways. Firstly, he projects the analysis into the twentieth century, and secondly, he extends it beyond Anglo-Saxon culture into Southeast Asia, specifically Burma (now Myanmar) and Vietnam, in his book *The Moral Economy of the Peasant.*

In his first volume on this theme, Scott analyzes institutions and practices of redistribution and charitable obligation in rural village life. He identifies both the norm of reciprocity and the right of subsistence as moral components of what he calls the "little tradition." In this phrase he is joining Thompson to the work of the anthropologist Robert Redfield, who sought to

> distinguish the beliefs and practices of the folk strata of an agrarian civilization from that of its elite. More or less in keeping with Redfield's concepts, we may define the little tradition as "the distinctive patterns of belief and behavior which are valued by the peasantry of an agrarian society"; the great tradition is the corresponding patterns among the society's elite. (Scott 1977: 7–8)

As Scott makes clear in his later work, the "little tradition" differs in detail from place to place but is shared in significant ways by all peasant cultures generally (see his comments on the modern peasant movement, La Vía Campesina, in Scott 2005: 397).

Scott is often mistaken for an anthropologist himself, but he was actually trained as a political scientist. This would explain why his book on peasant culture in Southeast Asia could be written from the libraries of Europe (Paris and London). It also explains why he begins his exploration of subsistence with an analysis of exploitation. He was trying to explain the social and economic preconditions of peasant unrest. For him it is obvious that the exponents of the "great tradition" in an agrarian society live on the surplus economic value they have extracted from the peasant class through taxes, rent, tithes and so forth. He also observes that when the manner of this extraction violates local custom or when it becomes excessive, it will be resisted as unjust. Even though the ruling, dominant or aristocratic class is not equal in power or social status to the rural, peasant or subordinate class, there are limits to what the poor will tolerate. "Custom and the subsistence needs of villagers thus establish moral ceilings on the economic claims which the great tradition may impose on subordinate classes" (Scott 1977: 16).

For Scott, exploitation is first of all a relationship—a relationship between individuals, groups or institutions—because the existence of someone being exploited implies the existence of an exploiter. Secondly, it is an unjust relationship. Scott actually uses the word "unfair" (Scott 1976: 158), but I think "unjust" is a better word because it better expresses the notion that the relationship is an extreme one. The presence of injustice implies a norm of justice, and so we have a pattern of economic relationships being described and resisted on moral grounds—a moral economy. Scott is not prepared to go far beyond that limited schematic because "ultimately, such disputes over what is exploitative and what is not are appeals to a normative tradition and not matters to be settled by empirical inquiry" (Scott 1976: 159). However, it is enough for him to be able to discern what constitutes the peasant's view of a decent landlord and a decent state. His reading of the Southeast Asian context indicates that structural changes during the colonial period permitted elites and the state to increase their exploitation of peasant groups and thereby violate the moral economy of the poor (Scott 1976: 157).

Scott's notion of exploitation contains three elements. He attends to the "relational or exchange quality" of social relations. He seeks out the "shared human needs" that the people involved expect from these relationships, and he works from the "actual notions of fair value" that prevail in the context (Scott 1976: 165).

Subsistence

The possibility of a universal character to moral economy rests on the existence of universally shared needs. In the case of peasant culture around the word, the need to assure subsistence can be accepted as universal. The consciousness of this as a moral economy may not be universal, because the consciousness appears as a response to threat. From Thompson's point of view, consciousness of the moral economy comes into existence in answer to the danger posed by the expansion of free-market ideology or the market economy or (beneath the mask) capitalism. Of course, no particular peasant group is born into a universal society. Rather, they are born into a specific culture and society, with specific expectations and relationships. They inherit a particular history, set of moral values and shared customary obligations. However, that does not invalidate the claim that they may also share a moral universe and a common notion of justice:

> To say that people are born into society is not to deny their capacity to create new forms and break old ones; it is merely to recall that they do not walk out on an empty stage and make up their lines at random. (Scott 1976: 166)

Scott observes the principle of subsistence in the social pressure exerted by the poor on the relatively well-off within the village, to be generous to their less fortunate neighbours. He describes this as one of the central characteristics of Southeast Asian village life. He also observes it in the preference for social arrangements that minimize the dangers of falling into destitution. He compares this pattern to areas of pre-industrial Europe where:

> The right to subsistence took concrete form in the doctrine of the "just price" tied to wages and in the practice of the Russian *mir* [an ancient form of peasant community] whose members redistributed land at regular intervals in accordance with family size. (Scott 1976: 177)

Where the moral norm of the right to subsistence is violated by the elite, a kind of implicit social contract is understood to have been violated. Then, violence by the peasant class is sanctioned if it is aimed at re-establishing the moral foundation of the social order. In a later book, Scott tells a story about peasants in nineteenth-century Prussia that has eerie similarities to the tale of the Scottish crofters:

> Prussian peasants and proletarians in the 1830s, beleaguered by dwarf holdings and wages below subsistence, responded by emigration or by poaching wood, fodder, and game on a large scale. The pace of "forest crime" rose as wages declined, as provisions became more expensive, and where emigration was more difficult; in 1836 there were 207,000 prosecutions in Prussia, 150,000 of which were for forest offences. They were supported by a mood of popular complicity that originated in earlier traditions of free access to forests, but the poachers cared little whether the rabbits or firewood they took came from the land of their particular employer or landlord. Thus, the reaction to an appropriation in one sphere may lead its victims to exploit small openings available elsewhere that are perhaps more accessible and less dangerous. (1985: 35)

When Scott published his *Moral Economy of the Peasant*, he was often asked where he had done his fieldwork. His embarrassed response indicating that no field work was involved generated what he called "anthropology envy," and led to two years on the Muda Plain in Malaysia, resulting in the publication of *Weapons of the Weak* in 1985 (Scott 2005: 396). Here he describes in detail the life of a village he names "Sedaka." This is a village that lived through the green revolution of the 1960s and 1970s, when pesticides and herbicides were introduced along with higher yielding crops. This allowed for the possibility of two harvests in a single year and, along with other technical innovations, replaced manual labour with mechanized labour. Social relations were under stress as landlords moved to rent out larger plots of land to new tenants from outside the village and as they began to demand that rents be paid before the harvest came in. Financial support from the government was manipulated to benefit the most influential families, again leaving the poorest increasingly disadvantaged. The most marginalized peasants found it increasingly difficult to provide for their families. While they may not have been starving, they had difficulty participating in the ritual events of village life that helped define their standing in the community. Just like the Scottish crofters, a limited land base makes self-support difficult and focuses attention on opportunities for wage labour.

One of those opportunities is created by a village gate. The gate prevents trucks from entering the village. In monsoon season, it prevents the muddy path from being destroyed, or deeply rutted, by heavily laden vehicles. In consequence, trucks must unload their cargo of lumber, bricks, metal roofing and furniture, and these would now be carried into the village. In the dry season, a fee of M$3 would be collected to open the gate and the truck allowed to pass. These fees would be collected into a community fund used to repair the road from the previous rainy season. This is an example of the community acting collectively to ensure environmental sustainability. Heavy trucks do much more damage than foot traffic, oxen or even small motorcycles.

Sustainability
We refer to the social dimension of sustainability as sufficiency. If agriculture or wage labour cannot produce enough resources to feed, clothe and shelter a family, the family will not be sustainable. Its members will starve or die of exposure or disease. In Sedaka, at harvest time, workers would be hired to haul sacks of harvested rice ("paddy") back to the gate and it would then be trucked to a mill in a nearby town. "The potential earnings for a villager were significant. It is not uncommon for a young man to earn as much as M$150 during the normal harvest and now, with double-cropping, such earnings were doubled" (Scott 1985: 213). The gate served as a collective mechanism of financial redistribution in order to ensure a sufficient living.

Equity
In *The Moral Economy of the Peasant*, Scott identifies the norms of subsistence and reciprocity as norms of the moral economy. In subsequent work he does not develop this normative perspective but rather goes on to describe and analyze the various techniques used by oppressed peoples to resist their exploitation. Short of outright rebellion, he describes these techniques as the "weapons of the weak." The terms he uses to identify these weapons are metaphors of the theatre. Scott distinguishes between speech and action that takes place "onstage" from those that take place "offstage." Onstage speech takes place when all the actors are in role. The roles are defined by class and culture so that the peasant is required by custom to show deference to the landlord, who is in turn required by religious obligation to give a small percentage of his non-operative capital as a gift to feed the poor. Offstage conversations take place in circumstances where the actors are not required to censor themselves—the poor with their families or the elites in their clubs. A comparison of these "transcripts" reveals the gap between what the actors say and what they really believe. I will come back to this notion in a later chapter, but for now I want to use these terms to continue the normative discussion.

One of the moral norms Scott points to is the concept of "fairness." It is already implied in the discussion of justice and exploitation. He also sees it revealed when tenants meet together out of earshot of the landlords. When landlords and tenants are together, when they are onstage, they use terms for sharecropping and tenancy that emphasize fairness or equity in these exchanges. However, when tenants are offstage, they are cynical and mocking of the terms of transaction. Scott concludes (1985: 40) that the tenants do not actually consider the relationship as fair but rather are forced to acquiesce because of the power imbalance:

> What are we to make of lower-class religious sects (the Quakers in 17th century England, Saminists in 20th century Java, to name only two of many) that abandon the use of honorifics to address their social betters and insist instead on low forms of address or on using words like "friend" or "brother" to describe everyone. Is this not telling evidence that the elite's libretto for the hierarchy of nobility and respect is, at the very least, not sung word for word by its subjects?

The concept of equity includes fairness and is related to the concept of equality, but is not the same as equality. An equitable relationship is one that is in balance, whereas an equal relationship is one between two parties that are the same. In Scott's rural Malaysian village, the people are manifestly unequal. Some have much more land than others. Some have more privileged access to the resources of the state, and some are accorded more prestige and honour than others. However, the distribution of work, of land, of rice and loans and charity is carried out within a complex set of obligations that are determined by notions of fairness. In a time of significant social and economic change, the understanding of these obligations is also changing and this leads to various grievances. One of the complaints has to do with a lack of generosity. The poor complain of "stinginess" and "tightfistedness" on the part of the well-off. "The rich were generous... before. We could ask for help.... Now its hard to ask for their assistance. Now they 'watch their pennies'" (Scott 1985: 17).

One of the ways in which villagers enforce the moral norm of equity is by defending or undermining reputations. When someone is described as "greedy" they are sometimes also described as being "without shame": "For it is shame, that concern for the good opinion of one's neighbours and friends, which circumscribes behaviour within the moral boundaries created by shared values. A man without shame is, by definition, capable of anything" (Scott 1985: 17).

The second complaint is one of arrogance and pride. "If the charge of stinginess implies the denial of generosity, of help, the charge of arrogance implies the denial of the conceptual equality of villagers" (Scott 1985: 195). I would describe this "conceptual equality" as a concept of moral equality.

Even though the villagers are manifestly unequal in material goods and power, the complaint reveals an underlying notion of moral equality indicating that each member has equal claim to membership in the community and to the rights that accompany that membership. One of those rights is the right to make a claim on the resources of the rich in times of extreme need. All rights imply obligations. If I have a right to make a claim on a community, the community has an obligation to honour that claim. If the rich refuse that claim, it is either because they lack generosity or because they have put themselves outside the community proper.

Of course, material self-interest can motivate the rich to minimize inequalities in order to minimize their obligations. So, too, material self-interest can motivate the poor to maximize inequality in order to maximize their claims. "What we observe, in brief, is not some trivial difference of opinion over the facts, but rather the confrontation of two social constructions of the facts, each designed and employed to promote the interest of a different class" (Scott 1985: 204). Having said that, the argument and the acknowledgment of the behaviour mean that there is, at least, a shared moral norm of equity in community relations, with its attendant rights and obligations. A rejection of that norm is a rejection of the bonds of solidarity with the rest of the community.

Solidarity
Scott writes of a norm of reciprocity, but I think the concept of solidarity is a more robust and useful term for our purposes. Reciprocity implies a balancing of accounts over time. You do this for me and I will do this for you. It is sometimes used to describe contractual relationships. Solidarity includes this notion but also goes beyond it. In larger or more complex systems, where the balancing compensation may come from a stranger or may not be needed so never come at all, people search for different words. "Mutuality" is sometimes used as a substitute and Scott uses this term as well. Solidarity can include the notion of mutuality, though mutuality also contains a notion of caring for the other that implies a more intimate connection between individuals than possible in a complex society.

In the story of the village gate, we see the principle of solidarity played out. The community enforces the village gate for environmental reasons, with a reciprocity that benefits everyone, and also for reasons of sufficiency. The poor benefit from the increased wages resulting when paddy brokers are forced to wait at the gate for sacks of rice to be brought to them. When a rich landlord or tenant takes down the gate at harvest time, it is solidarity with the poor that has been broken, and it becomes a matter of struggle as to whether the community has the cultural and ideological coherence to enforce the moral norm.

Another form of solidarity is observed when one group of threshers refuses to act as strike-breakers and undercut another group who are negotiating with the landlord. Similarly, it can be seen when a landlord tries to raise the rent on land, and other villagers refuse to bid on the tenancy so as not to disadvantage the original tenant.

> No extravagant claims can be made for this sanctioned self-restraint, inasmuch as it operates only within the confines of the village itself, and even in this context its operation is narrowly circumscribed. It does, however, prevent the most damaging excesses of competition between the poor for the few opportunities available. (Scott 1985: 261)

The practical impact of this solidarity can be observed in economic studies of land rents in the region.

> Rent levels in general, even for non-kinship tenancies, are somewhat lower than a purely economic analysis would predict. The difference, while it is not large, is at least in part attributable to the small degree of local mutuality the poor have managed to create. (Scott 1985: 264)

This solidarity can also be described as intra-class solidarity. It is the solidarity of tenants with other tenants and of wage labourers with other wage labourers. The norm of solidarity also applies across classes, but again we tend to use different language to describe it. One term used to describe this second kind of solidarity is the term "social contract."

Social Contract and the Moral Economy

In Thompson's story of the English crowd in the eighteenth century, we saw direct action by the poor to defend their interests. They acted in solidarity with each other and made claims against the rich landlords who had broken solidarity with the poor. They acted to ensure they had sufficient food and they charged the elites with fundamental injustice. The inequities were also illegal, according to their memory of royal statutes.

In Scott's story of Sedaka on the Muda plain of Malaysia, we also have a remembered village and a remembered economy. The villagers remember when rents were paid after the harvest and were adjusted if the harvest was weak. They remember the times before mechanization when harvest work was plentiful and they were always invited to the village feasts. They remember in this way because they find themselves on the defensive as the market economy expands and continues to erode the social contract on which their expectations rest. The social contract contains the moral norms and cultural practices that constitute the moral economy. If, in our time, the global spread of capitalist market economy is becoming a universal experience, and if the moral economy becomes visible at the last stage of this historical process (Thompson 1978: 149) at which time ordinary people rise up to defend it, then I think we can observe some common elements of a moral economy:

> The defense and elaboration of a social contract that has been abrogated by capitalist development is perhaps the most constant ideological theme of the peasant and the early capitalist worker— from the Levellers and Diggers of the English Revolution to the craftsmen and weavers threatened with extinction to the "Captain Swing" rebels fighting the use of the threshing machines. The same defense of beleaguered traditional rights is found at the core of popular intellectual attacks on capitalism by figures as ideologically diverse as Cobbett, Paine, and Carlyle. (Scott 1985: 347)

In this chapter I have identified the four principles of moral economy as sufficiency, sustainability, equity and solidarity. Thompson described the moral economy from the perspective of England in the eighteenth century. James Scott described the moral economy from the perspective of Southeast Asia in the twentieth century. Marc Edelman, writing in *American Anthropologist* in 2005, updated Scott's 1976 *The Moral Economy of the Peasant* by reviewing the emergence of anti-globalization protests, particularly those of the transnational peasant movement La Vía Campesina. Edelman convincingly demonstrates that the concern for subsistence continues to be paramount in the contemporary critique of international trade agreements and the World Trade Organization (WTO). Removal of domestic subsidies and the institution of new trading rules that dismantle institutions like marketing boards destroy the economic base of small peasant farmers. This has the cumulative effect of shifting the emphasis of agricultural production to an export market and therefore undermining rural subsistence economies that rely on domestic production for domestic consumption.

Scott was very complimentary about Edelman's analysis: "Marc Edelman's article made me proud once again that I had written *The Moral Economy of the Peasant*" (Scott 2005: 396). As Scott understands it, Edelman has interpreted the moral economy through Polanyi's notion of society's impulse for self-protection, otherwise known as the "double movement." The market failures described on a local scale by Thompson and Scott were answered in the twentieth century by systems of national social insurance, or the welfare state. Since the fall of the Berlin Wall in 1989, this particular form of the moral economy has been under relentless attack by supranational organizations like the WTO. In response, peasant movements have increasingly turned to international cooperation through vehicles like the La Vía

Campesina. Scott is sceptical that the international organization of farmers will be enough in the struggle to re-establish principles of moral economy:

> Some combination of power at the polling place, alliances with workers, and what is left of the national bourgeoisie… seem to be the most likely routes to blocking the clean sweep of neoliberal governance and preserving national food security and the communities of peasant producers. (Scott 2005: 397–8)

I will follow this lead and make one more extrapolation, and that is the extrapolation from farmers to all other workers and their communities. Though Thompson and Scott have focused on farming communities, Polanyi did not, and when Thompson shone the light on the eighteenth-century English crowd, he was actually profiling the majority of the population. In concluding this chapter I tell a story of a very contemporary community struggling for equity and sufficiency. The global market failure of 2008 and 2009 has provided fresh opportunity to understand the double movement of market threat and social self-preservation.

The Living Wage

The "living wage movement" started in the United States, in Baltimore in 1994 (Pollin and Luce 1998). From there it spread to many countries including the U.K., where it caught on in London, especially after a broad-based community coalition called London Citizens launched a campaign in 2001. It has spread from hospitals to the finance district and from universities to hotels. A special focus of it has been the upcoming London Olympics in 2012, and the campaign has secured agreements that all new jobs at the Olympic site will provide a living wage. According to one study, more than 6,000 workers have secured wage increases as a direct result of the campaign (Wills et al. 2009: 4).

The living wage is not the same as what is commonly called a minimum wage. The living wage is defined by the Family Budget Unit as "a wage that achieves an adequate level of warmth and shelter, a healthy palatable diet, social integration and avoidance of chronic stress for earners and their dependents" (GLA Economics 2009: 7). In England in 2008, the London living wage (LLW) was set 30 percent higher than the government-regulated national minimum wage (NMW). The Greater London Authority established in 2009 that 15 percent of all full-time and 47 percent of all part-time workers in London fell into the gap between the NMW and the LLW (GLA Economics 2009: 5).

It should come as no surprise that the cost of living differs from one place to another. Global corporations know this as a very practical matter.

They hire firms like Mercer International to do comparisons so they know that when they transfer a management employee from Washington DC to London, England, they will need to pay that employee 40 percent more for them to achieve the same standard of living. It is necessary for them to calculate the differential, because they need to offer enough inducement to ensure that employees are willing to be transferred and that they aren't hired away by a competitor at the other end. Of course, they don't transfer cleaning staff.

In 2005, a living wage organizing effort was started at Queen Mary, a college at the University of London, to improve the working conditions of contracted cleaning staff. Contracting out of services has been one of the strategies used by neo-liberal governments to reduce costs and fight union-ization. The workers moved from contractor to contractor as the contracts themselves were moved around. "The longest serving cleaners recall working for three different contractors in the past 15 years" (Wills et al. 2009: 6). In 2006, after widespread consultations involving faculty as well as administra-tors, Queen Mary committed to becoming the first living-wage campus in the U.K. In January 2008, administrators undertook to bring the cleaning staff back in-house, even though that was not what was initially requested. The effect of that move, however, was to dramatically improve terms and conditions of work.

Fears that the move would lead to dramatically increased costs were not well founded, and figures to date indicate that the in-house service has cost only slightly more than the service provided by contractors:

> Managers report that fewer staff, better supervision and higher productivity have reduced the predicted escalation of costs. Dean Curtis, the Chief Administrative Officer reported feeling "*perfectly happy*" and "*completely relaxed*" about the slight increase in costs, argu-ing that this was what "*we expected*." (Wills et al. 2009: 14)

This story serves as a contemporary example of a movement to defend sub-sistence as a right for all workers, not just those involved in agriculture. For our purposes it is even more significant that this struggle is seen and justified in plainly moral terms. Sarah Cowls, Deputy Academic Secretary of Queen Mary, expressed her support for the campaign in the following terms:

> [The college is] located in an area of deprivation. The cleaners live in the local area and the decision has an impact on the local com-munity. Queen Mary has to take a high moral standing because of the nature of what we do. If we are not going to do something like that, who is? I think it's very important that the University takes the lead in [this]. It's the right thing. (Wills et al. 2009: 31)

Many echoed this heart-felt support. Subsistence as a right for all workers does not mean that all workers will necessarily come under the "living wage" umbrella. However, in Greater London it does mean that almost 50 percent of part-time workers will come under this protection if the policy is fully implemented. The right to subsistence is a more serious issue if you are closer to the poverty line. The poor may be forced to claim it through civil disobedience, like the Scottish crofters, but they will be justified on the basis of an unashamedly moral argument—the argument for a moral economy.

Notes

1. Crofters were tenants of small land holdings; cottars were cottagers with no tenure, often descended from crofters who had been dispossessed by the clearances in the previous century. See Norton 1994: ix and Devine 1994: 235.
2. Wolseley had been named after Colonel Garnet Wolseley, a British officer who had come to Canada in 1870 to enforce federal authority in the face of the Red River (Northwest) Rebellion.

4. Embeddedness and Theories of Moral Economy

The Digital Economy

Have you ever downloaded music from the internet? Do you know anyone else who has? Have you ever sent a copy of a song you liked to a friend? When you did, were you sharing a treasured experience and giving a gift, or were you shoplifting and passing along stolen goods? Those are very different ways of characterizing the same activity, aren't they?

Joel Tenenbaum was sixteen years old in 2003 when he received a letter from Sony BMG Music Entertainment demanding $5,250 for seven songs he had downloaded through a file-sharing service on the internet. Joel was scared by this official and legal letter demanding payment so, with help from his parents, he sent along a cheque for $500 and explained that he was a high school student and couldn't afford anything more than that. They offered to settle for $3,500 and his cheque was returned.[1]

Joel graduated from high school and moved to Boston to attend university. Four years later he received a notice demanding that he appear in court. He was being sued for copyright infringement, along with some thirty thousand other people, by companies like Sony Music, Warner Brothers and Arista records, all coordinated by the Record Industry Association. Joel offered to settle for $5,000 but the record companies now wanted $10,500.

At this point a law professor offered to represent Joel in court. Charles Neeson holds the William F. Wed Chair in Law at Harvard University, where he is also the founder and co-director of the Birkman Center for Internet and Society. Professor Neeson believes that the internet is a digital version of the old common grazing lands of the seventeenth century. He believes the internet was started as an open domain but has recently been fenced off by investors who want to increase their profits through new exclusive property rights.

Joel lost his court case in the summer of 2009, as he expected. He was found guilty of downloading thirty songs and ordered to pay compensation of $22,500 per song—$675,000. He will appeal and if he loses again, he will declare bankruptcy. Is this an example of the law acting as it should (theft is prosecuted) and therefore ensuring that the economy remains embedded in society? Or is this an example of a gift being turned upside down so that social relationships are now restructured and embedded in economic relationships? How does this concept of embeddedness actually work?

The Always Embedded Economy

Earlier we considered how the discourse about ethics has become separated from that of economics in Western thought and practice. Through the work of E.P. Thompson we learned how ordinary people in eighteenth-century England rebelled against market-based innovations that failed to address their own needs for subsistence and sustainability, and how they relied on social solidarity to advance their claims for justice. With Thompson we learned to call this form of protest an invocation of the moral economy of the crowd, and with James Scott we learned that this type of resistance and reasoning was not confined to eighteenth-century England. It can also be found in other cultures at other times, such as Southeast Asia in the twentieth century. With Karl Polanyi we learned to relativize the principles of market economy, seeing them as characteristic of the formal economy as opposed to the substantive economy. We also learned to consider the rise of protest-based moral economy as an expression of the double movement of social self-protection against the corrosive effects of a supposedly self-regulating market system. Some authors have now taken this style of analysis in a new direction. Rather than restricting the concept of a moral economy to an ideal state of affairs (Powleson 1998) or to moments of social protest, these authors conceive of the moral economy as a discipline of inquiry. This shift is based on the idea that the economy is *always embedded* in society and there-fore the moral character of these economic relationships is always available for scrutiny. This represents a serious challenge to Polanyi's analysis and so deserves special attention. If the economy is always embedded, how can the relationship between economy and society be reversed? Does the presumption of an *always embedded economy* mean that the concept of the double movement is no longer credible?

Mark Granovetter is a sociologist who specializes in the study of social networks. In 1985 he wrote a highly influential article on the problem of em-beddedness. In that article he argues that all economic behaviour is embedded in social relationships, but this is meant in sociological terms, as referring to interpersonal relationships (friendships, family ties, other associations) and cultural expectations due to shared experiences or shared backgrounds. I would refer to this as informal versus formal embedding.

Granovetter divides his opponents into two camps. On the one side are inheritors of the utilitarian tradition, including classical and neo-classical economists, who assume that people always exhibit, and always have ex-hibited, rational (by which they mean materially self-interested) behaviour, which is only minimally affected by social relationships. He would describe these theorists as having an "under-socialized" view of human action.

On the other side are those identified with the substantivist school in anthropology, who argue that economic behaviour and institutions in the premodern period were so constrained by social relations that they cannot really be understood as independent. This school of thought, identified with Karl Polanyi, further argued that with modernity this situation was reversed— "instead of economic life being submerged in social relations, these relations became an epiphenomenon of the market" (Granovetter 1985: 482).

Granovetter tries to split the difference between these two positions. "My own view diverges from both schools of thought," he writes.

> I assert that the level of embeddedness of economic behaviour is lower in nonmarket societies than is claimed by substantivists and development theorists, and it has changed less with "moderization" than they believe; but I argue also that this level has always been and continues to be more substantial than is allowed for by formalists and economists. (Granovetter 1985: 482–3)

The biggest problem with Granovetter seems to be that other writers have tried to do with his arguments exactly what he said he was not trying to do. He wrote, "I make no claims for this analysis to answer large-scale questions about the nature of modern society or the sources of economic and political change." Rather he is simply trying to demonstrate that "all market processes are amenable to sociological analysis" (Granovetter 1985: 506). Indeed, even though he cites Polanyi in his early work, in a later writing he admitted, "I was not thinking about [Polanyi] when I wrote that paper" (Krippner, Granovetter & Block et al. 2004: 114). Actually, it was only after writing it that he was reminded of Polanyi's use of the concept many years ago, and so he decided to include a citation. For Granovetter, embeddedness is "a conceptual umbrella under which one should look into and think about what are the connections between economic activity and the social, the political, the institutional, the historical, the cultural elements that economic activity is mixed up with" (Krippner, Granovetter & Block et al. 2004: 133).

If Granovetter's understanding of embeddedness really is so far from Polanyi's, it begs the question of why his paper was so influential. Indeed, Granovetter himself remarked that if he had known how extensive the impact was going to be, "I would have taken more care to say there's more to life than the structure of social networks" (Krippner, Granovetter & Block 2004: 115). Three answers were offered up by different writers at a 2004 symposium. Nicole Biggart suggests that it had to do with the movement of academic sociologists onto business school faculties in the 1990s. Economists in business schools "assume a market" by which they mean a "logically perfect market" which "has no social relationships." Granovetter was useful to sociologists teaching in business schools because it provided an opportunity to think about markets as "something other than a conceptually empty category"—namely, as embedded (Biggart in Krippner, Granovetter & Block, 2004: 115).

Gillian Hart offers two additional explanations. First, in the 1990s there was a debate about the developmental state and the role of the state in the economy (Evans 1995). Neo-liberals argued that the East Asian miracle economies were market-led. The notion of embeddedness was used to shore up the counter-argument about the active role of the state in the context of Asia. Second, Robert Putnam published his book about social capital in 1993 and in 1995 Ismail Serageldin, the newly appointed vice-president for environmentally and socially sustainable development of the World Bank, published the first World Bank document to use that phrase. As an example of the double movement and in reaction to the criticism of neoliberalism, a static notion of embeddedness is employed by the World Bank (Hart in Krippner, Granovetter & Block 2004: 123).

So, there are two routes away from Polanyi. One follows the work of Max Weber and gets instituted within the World Bank, and the second follows the theories of Karl Marx and questions the slippages and contradictions that emerge within neoliberalism in the 1980s and 1990s. In both cases the concept of embeddedness is embraced and is traced back not to Polanyi, but to Granovetter.

Bernard Barber was a distinguished professor of sociology at Columbia University. In 1995 he responded to Granovetter by seeking to provide a history of the concept of "embeddedness" and by providing a better general understanding of the term. In order to provide that improved understanding, he starts with an overview of what is meant by the "market."

The Market as Utopia and Ideology

In relation to the discipline of economics, Barber's focus on history is designed to overcome "the common tendency among economists and others to what I have called 'the absolutization of the market'" (Barber 1995: 388). According to Barber, mainstream economists have simply assumed the existence of a market economy and the economizing behaviour one finds there; they no longer consider it as simply one form of economy among others and one pattern of behaviour among others. He can find no detailed elaboration of the concept of the "market" in the *International Encyclopedia of the Social Sciences,* for example. It is mentioned only briefly by Adam Smith in *The Wealth of Nations* and even more briefly by Karl Marx in his three-volume *Capital.* Even Joseph Schumpeter's 1,200-page *History of Economic Analysis* is silent on the matter. The market has now become paradigmatic. Insofar as it now seems singular, it can appear unassailable.

Barber follows the sociologist Karl Mannheim, who "defined ideology as a conservative belief that justifies the existing social order, and utopia as a revolutionary belief that distorts social reality in order to justify social change." From this perspective, he understands Polanyi as saying that the "concept of the market was formerly a Utopia, but now it has become an establishment ideology" (Barber 1995: 390).

Barber views Polanyi as the father of the "embeddedness" concept, and when Polanyi described the market as having become "disembedded" from society, he was contrasting market exchange with the two other forms of economic exchange which were much more embedded, namely reciprocity and redistribution. Barber thinks this concept is not very well developed by Polanyi and finds that unsurprising. The market system was created in an incremental fashion, and the theorists and ideologists who justified it also did so in a "bits-and-pieces" manner (Barber 1995: 393). Barber finds the concept of embeddedness to be a useful one but disagrees with Polanyi that market exchange can ever be fully disembedded. Since market exchange is only one form of social exchange, and since "all social interaction is determined in part, but only in part, by norms and values," then market exchange must also be determined in part by norms and values. "Each type of social interaction is also and always interdependent with a whole variety of partly independent social-structural, cultural-structural, and personality-structural variables of the social system" (Barber 1995: 395). In this he occupies similar ground to moral economists like Andrew Sayer. "Our strong proposition, contrary to Polanyi's, is that *all* economies are inescapably embedded" (Barber 400). Where Polanyi is at pains to demonstrate how market exchange has superseded and displaced reciprocity and redistribution, Barber aims to demonstrate how reciprocity and redistribution continue to exist alongside market exchange. Marcel Mauss's work on "gift exchange" (*The Gift* 1925) and Richard Titmuss's work on blood donation (*The Gift Relationship* 1971) are both examples of contemporary forms of reciprocity based on status not contract (Henry Maine, Ancient Law 1861). He also identifies the large systems of economic redistribution, through welfare and income tax legislation, that function in the otherwise capitalist economies of the West (Barber 1995: 397).

Barber's argument shares a great deal with that of Granovetter. Both are critical of mainstream economic analysis, and especially of rational choice theorists, for ignoring the sociological dimension of their work. Both want to make a stronger case for the discipline of economic sociology. Both believe economic actions are embedded in social norms and values. "One can hardly doubt the existence of some such generalized morality," Granovetter writes, "without it you would be afraid to give the gas station attendant a 20-dollar bill when you bought only five dollars' worth of gas" (Granovetter 1985: 489). It helps to remember that Granovetter was writing in 1985. How much gas could you buy for $5 today? Barber also praises Granovetter for insisting on "the embeddedness of all economic action in non-economic social relations" (Barber 1995: 406).

While Barber tries to strengthen the theoretical foundations of the concept of "embeddedness" by disagreeing with Polanyi, he also disagrees with Mark Granovetter. Barber finds Granovetter wanting in his appreciation of the way that economies are located in larger social systems. He is also critical of Granovetter's silence on the question of alternative economic systems and the alternative behaviours (like reciprocity and redistribution) that coexist alongside market exchange. Most importantly though, Barber is critical of Granovetter's use of a "network of interpersonal relations model" instead of a social systems model to describe the bed in which we always find the economy. "Granovetter says that economic behavior is embedded in 'social structure,' and for him social structure apparently means only networks of interpersonal relations. There is no specification of the several different social and cultural structures that make up the larger social system" (Barber 1995: 407). What is missing are social structures like race, gender and class; symbolic systems like religion, philosophy, ideology and art; and all forms of cultural structures.

Barber's analysis is clear and persuasive. He calls for a proper history of the concept of the market and he establishes inconsistencies in Polanyi's use of the term even as he acknowledges Polanyi's innovations. However, missing from the analysis is a sympathetic analysis of the concept of "disembedding." People do experience powerfully the inversion of the relationship between the social and the economic. To say that society is now determined by the economy, instead of the reverse, strikes many people as a true description of their experience. If the economy has not been disembedded from culture and social structure, then from what has it been disembedded? Insofar as the market system now occupies a dominant position in action and in discourse and is resisting the protective response of the double movement, it makes sense to say that the market economy functions as an ideology to protect the status quo. Below, we will see that according to some authors this oper-

---

"SOMEBODY HAS BEEN LYING IN MY BED!" said the Great, Huge Bear, in his great, rough, gruff voice.

And little Silver-hair had pulled the bolster of the Middle Bear out of its place.

"Somebody has been lying in my bed!" said the Middle Bear in his middle voice.

And when the Little, Small, Wee Bear came to look at his bed, there was the bolster in its place; and the pillow in its place on the bolster; and upon the pillow was little Silver-hair's pretty head—which was not in its place, for she had no business there.

"Somebody has been lying on my bed—and here she is!" said the Little, Small, Wee Bear, in his little small, wee voice." — Joseph Cundall, "The Three Bears," in A Treasury of Pleasure Books for Young People, 1856

ates precisely at the level of ideas. But insofar as the market economy is still gaining ground and still enclosing new territory, like the digital commons, it also makes sense to describe it as utopian for it continues to distort lived reality in order to reshape society in its own image.

Taking the Market for Granted

Greta Krippner, a sociologist teaching at the University of Michigan, is a critic of Granovetter and those who have adopted his understanding of embeddedness. Like Barber, her issue is that even when people are defending their use of embeddedness, or trying to strengthen the concept, they inevitably reinforce the idea of the market as a socially empty concept upon which social content is imposed from outside.

> Quite paradoxically, the basic intuition that markets are socially embedded—while containing an important insight—has led economic sociologists to take the market itself for granted. As a result, economic sociology has done scarcely better than economics in elaborating the concept of the market as a theoretical object in its own right. (Krippner 2001: 776)

Although Krippner says that she knew Granovetter was not relying on Polanyi when he wrote his 1985 paper ("I think I was aware of that when I read your piece"—Krippner, Granovetter & Block 2004: 125) she still wrote in 2001 that "it is well known that he drew the concept from Polanyi's various mid-century writings" (Krippner 2001: 778).

Krippner is a defender of Polanyi, who she understands as having developed a dynamic, as opposed to static, view of the economy and its relationship to society. She sees him as wanting to expose the standard view of market society as an ideology that falsely presents hunger and gain as timeless and universal forces that determine the character of society. Krippner wonders if some disciples of Polanyi "have (unwittingly) subverted Polanyi's own vision of market society by re-inforcing the asocial market construct?" (Krippner 2001: 787). She thinks some interpreters of Polanyi fail to remember that he operated on several different levels simultaneously. On the one hand he was trying to demonstrate that the self-regulating market was not a trans-historical category—that it was particular to nineteenth-century Britain. On the other hand he was also trying to demonstrate that it was a utopian, political project. If carried to its logical conclusion the results would be devastating socially, so all parts of society rose up to constrain it—hence the double movement.

In defending Polanyi, Krippner also argues that "there are limits to the extent to which Polanyi can be said to have endorsed a truly disembedded view of the market" (Krippner 781). Polanyi, in her view, says that market society could not exist for long without significant political intervention.

This raises two issues relevant to this discussion. The first is the meaning of the term "disembedded." Let us concede that the concept is underdeveloped in Polanyi and it may even be used by him in confusing ways. What Krippner is saying is that market economies can only become disembedded for very short periods of time and then not by accident but only by dint of extraordinary political force. This is helpful because it underscores how individual markets and the whole market system are embedded politically. It also points to how a market economy can become disembedded *in the transition from one regime of political regulation to another*. At the time of writing in 2010, we are living through the aftermath of one of the worst market failures of the last century. There is a direct line between the deregulation of the financial sector and the devastation of people's livelihoods. There are many proposals to re-regulate the financial sector, including a movement in some places to nationalize the banks (Sanger 2009). These represent a new form of political embeddedness. The period of time between the end of the old era of financial regulation, through the new era of deregulation, to a new era of financial regulation may be shorter than thirty years. But the crisis in which the financial markets failed and people lost their homes and jobs may only have lasted a year or two. Even then, the market economy was only partly disembedded, never fully. This is consistent with Fred Block's comments that "these political structurings of markets have limited time frames. They can work for 20, 30, 40 years, then they come into crisis, and enter into periods when they need renewal" (Krippner, Granovetter & Block 2004: 118).

The second issue raised has to do with the term "market society." Polanyi used the term to describe the extreme form called for by the laissez-faire liberals of the nineteenth century. This was the society that was supposed to be run as an adjunct of the market economy. However, the terminology seems to have changed so that people now use the term to describe the current period in Western society in which the market is the dominant institution, but the market economy has been re-embedded in a society governed to varying degrees by liberal assumptions. You could say that market society now represents a society of "embedded liberalism" (Ruggie 1982: 393).

Although Krippner is primarily focused on debates within sociology, she has carefully analyzed the ways in which theorists struggling with the concept of embeddedness have imported a continuing separation of the economic from the social:

> It is [my] premise... that we will be unable to grasp markets fully as constitutive of and constituted by social relations until the concept of embedded-ness is liberated from intellectual antecedents that

presuppose the separation of economy from broader realms of
social life. (Krippner 2001: 798)

Fred Block is also a sociologist and an important interpreter of Karl
Polanyi's work. He has written an introduction to the latest English language
edition of *The Great Transformation* (Polanyi 2001), and he has argued that
if we are to take Polanyi seriously, his work must be subjected to serious
critical review. Block has done this himself, most obviously with his critical
revision of Polanyi's assessment of the Speenhamland system and the Poor
Law reform of 1834 (Block & Somers 2003). Block has written many times
on Polanyi (see for example Block & Somers 1984; Krippner, Granovetter
& Block 2004; Block & Somers 2005), and his thinking has developed over
time.

Block emphasizes Polanyi's analysis of the utopian character of nineteenth-century liberals' project to create a system of self-regulating markets
and to embed society within this now autonomous economy. Market liberals
pushed their project at every opportunity but they could not succeed because
the cost of achieving it was the destruction of society. Their success required
self-regulating markets for labour, land and money, Polanyi's "fictitious commodities." But these key markets could not be self-regulating. Since "actually
existing market economies are dependent upon the state to manage the supply and demand for the fictitious commodities, there can be no analytically
autonomous economy" (Block 2004: 282). Block understands Polanyi to say
that all economies are always embedded in social relations and institutions,
and that even the newly formed market society depends upon coercion com-
ing from outside the economy per se, from the state.

Now it must be accepted that this is an emendation of Polanyi's concept
(Block might call it a development of the concept). Block recognizes that
Polanyi has often been read as saying that in market societies, the economy
has been effectively disembedded. He references Bernard Barber in this
regard and acknowledges that "there are contradictory arguments loose in
the text" (Block 2004: 294).

In my own case, I have read Polanyi in just this way, as arguing that the
creation of market economy (based on a self-regulating system of markets)
caused the economy to become disembedded from society and reversed the
relationship, causing society to be embedded in the economy (Lind 1995b).
The mechanism for this disembedding, reversal and re-embedding was the
reorganization of labour, land and money based on the principles of price-
setting markets. Between specific economic behaviours and specific social
relations and institutions, the relationship changes.

Polanyi did also suggest this notion of disembedding. He described
how the organization of labour and land and money according to market

principles caused an "economic sphere" to come into existence in a new way. This sphere was "sharply delineated from other institutions in society." It was embodied in a "distinct and separate sphere" that had "the effect of making the 'rest' of society dependent upon that sphere" (Polanyi 1947: 111). I agree with Block that one of Polanyi's achievements is his insistence that "Man's [sic] economy is, as a rule, submerged in his social relations" (even though Polanyi himself seems to think he was only retrieving an insight from Aristotle). However, the sentence that follows the one just quoted, from Polanyi's 1947 article in *Commentary*, requires a stronger explanation than Block provides. Polanyi goes on to say that "the change from this to a society which was, on the contrary, submerged in the economic system was an entirely novel development" (Polanyi 1947: 112). In the context of an argument against economic determinism as a general law for all societies, Polanyi says it even more boldly: "instead of the economic system being embedded in social relationships, these relationships were now embedded in the economic system" (Polanyi 1947: 114).

Now, if the logic of Polanyi's argument really points in the direction of the always embedded economy, as Block and others argue, one needs to ask: why would Polanyi suggest the concept of the disembedded economy at all? What was he trying to explain? If we go back to the *Great Transformation*, we find that he was trying to explain what he described as a "catastrophe" and the arrival of a "new institutional mechanism."

> We submit that an avalanche of social dislocation, surpassing by far that of the enclosure period, came down upon England; that this catastrophe was the accompaniment of a vast movement of economic improvement; that an entirely new institutional mechanism was starting to act on Western society; that its dangers, which cut to the quick when they first appeared, were never really overcome; and that the history of nineteenth century civilization consisted largely of such a mechanism…. but the new creed was utterly materialistic and believed that all human problems could be resolved given an unlimited amount of material commodities. (Polanyi 1957: 40)

So, Polanyi is trying to describe an experience of massive social dislocation and a period of great human misery. If the economy is always embedded, how then do we explain the social catastrophe? If the economy is always embedded, what do we do with the concept of disembeddedness? The concept is trying to describe something real.

It seems to me we don't have to abandon the concept altogether, and we are given glimpses of how to retain it in Polanyi, Block and the rest. One glimpse has to do with the concept of "market society." It is a quite reasonable reading of Polanyi to say that he thought market society already existed in the nineteenth century (Polanyi 1957: 230). Indeed, he thought of market society as one where society was embedded in a market economy and not the other way around (i.e., the economy was disembedded), and he expected this to be overcome in the second half of the twentieth century. Indeed he thought the market economy was already on its way out at the end of the World War II:

> Meanwhile, the first phase of the Machine Age has run its course, It involved an organization of society that derived its name from its central institution, the market. This system is on the downgrade. (Polanyi 1947: 110)

Who's on Top?

If market society is a society with a disembedded economy, then this dis-embeddedness would have lasted more than a hundred years from Polanyi's point of view—from at least the reform of the Poor Law in 1834 until 1947. Maybe it is enough to say that where society is organized along capitalist lines, where price-setting markets determine the cost of labour, land and money, the term "market society" is a good description. (I agree that there are "varieties of capitalism"; see e.g., Hall & Soskice 2001) This is a situation where market economy dominates society and the institution of the market becomes the dominant institution in society. So, one meaning of the term "embeddedness" concerns the dynamic of dominance and subordination. Where social relationships are subordinate to economic relationships we can say the economy has been disembedded because it now has a dominant position with regard to society. The term "market society" describes this inversion in the case of Western, capitalist society.

However, there are other meanings of "embeddedness" also in use. The very word evokes a cluster of images. A person lies in a bed. A fossil is embedded in a stratum of limestone. A reporter for CNN is embedded with the U.S. Army in Iraq. Partly the image has to do with the notions of foreground and background. A person lying down is seen against the background of the bed. The museum organizes a display of fossils, not a display of limestone. The limestone is merely the bed in which the fossil was discovered. Our focus is on the fossil. However, the image of the reporter embedded with the Army carries additional meanings. The concept of an embedded reporter is criticized because the reporter is no longer free. They only go where the Army goes, and the reader or viewer only reads or sees events from the Army's point of view. The image of "embeddedness" carries with it notions of constraint, limitation and regulation. The fossil is preserved precisely because it has been immobilized, fatally so.

The market economy requires legal and political regulation in order to function effectively. In this way we can say that the market economy is always embedded in some form of regulation. As Abraham Rotstein used to say to his students, "No economy is born naked in the world—every economy is born in a society much as every child is born of a mother. It is expected that the norms and requirements of each would influence the other" (personal correspondence). This is consistent with Block's analysis and re-interpretation of Polanyi. Polanyi saw that the effort to create a utopian self-regulating economy represented a grave threat to society. This threat provoked a counter-tendency he called a "counter movement"—the effort to protect society from the market. This movement to protect interfered with the functioning and expansion of market self-regulation and so produced a series of crises leading to the collapse of nineteenth-century civilization. Polanyi writes that these crises "forced the development of the market system into a definite groove" (Block & Polanyi 2003: 294).

Block re-reads Polanyi as arguing that the spontaneous efforts to protect society actually re-embedded the economy—that some degree of embeddedness is always required. The implication is that this what is meant by "a definite groove":

> But what actually happens... is... through the whole history of market society, the strength of protection effectively embeds the economy... functioning market societies must maintain some threshold level of embeddedness or else risk social and economic disaster. (Block & Polanyi 2003: 295)

The Threat of an Idea

We could say here that it is the idea of a disembedded economy that is most threatening, if it provides an intellectual justification for removing social protections.

What Block highlights first and foremost in Polanyi's analysis is the significance of state action. The creation of competitive markets requires deliberate and ongoing action by the state. The competitive market for labour was formally created by the 1834 Poor Law reform. This was followed by various acts of Parliament, like the Factory Act to regulate working conditions and the use of child labour. The market for land was regulated in order to assure a reliable supply of food. The market for money required its own infrastructure of embeddedness in the form of central banks to regulate the banking system and smooth out the growth of the money supply, but these didn't come into existence until the last quarter of the nineteenth century (Block & Polanyi 2003: 296). Though Adam Smith expected the common good to be achieved by the actions of an invisible hand coordinating all the self-interested actions of individuals in a self-regulating market, all of the above are examples of society acting, as it needed to, to force those same actions into socially beneficial ends. But these are all actions of the state.

In this way, Block introduces the idea of "levels of embeddedness," the idea that markets can be more or less embedded. This is his response to the criticism leveled by Greta Krippner that his suggestion of a society with greater or lesser degrees of "marketness" re-introduces the idea of a market devoid of social character. (Later on, Block will introduce another possibility.)

In their 2005 comparison of the English Poor Law reform of 1834 and the U.S. welfare reform of 1996, Fred Block and Margaret Somers introduce the concept of ideational embeddedness. This is a set of ruling ideas and metaphors that "shape, structure and change market regimes" (Block & Somers 2005: 260). In both the early nineteenth century and the late twentieth century they trace the rise of what they call "market fundamentalism." Quoting Pierre Bourdieu, they see these two cases as examples of theory-driven legislation that justify themselves by changing reality to reflect abstract models (Bourdieu 1998: 95). "It follows that even the most aggressive 'free market' reforms do not disembed markets but simply re-embed them in different institutional arrangements" (Block & Somers 2005: 264).

So the triumph of market fundamentalism represents neither the disembedding of the economy from society nor even the absence of ideational embeddedness. Rather,

> it is simply a different ideational regime, one that embeds markets in a story about how they are self-regulating natural entities and thus must be set free. The struggle between institutional pragmatism and market fundamentalism was not over whether but which body of ideas would do the embedding. (Block & Somers 2005: 281)

Embeddedness: Levels versus Varieties

More recently, Kurtulus Gemici argued that Karl Polanyi uses the term "embeddedness" in two very different ways, and that this has led to endless debates about "what Polanyi really meant." He considers these to be sterile debates and asks instead whether these two concepts are both useful. In the first place he argues that embeddedness is used by Polanyi "as an analytical construct to discern the changing place of economy in society throughout human history." He uses the concept "to specify the degree to which economy is 'separated' from the rest of society. Here, embeddedness is a historical variable; the market economy is an anomaly since it is the first 'disembedded' economic system in history" (Gemici 2008: 6). Used in this way it can be conceived as a gradational concept, with different levels of embeddedness being observed at different times.

In the second instance, Polanyi conceives of embeddedness as a "methodological principle positing that economy and society can only be analyzed through a holistic approach; economic life can be analyzed only through the examination of how it forms a part of social relations and institutions" (Gemici 2008: 7). In this case, we are not dealing with an analytical concept nor are we dealing with a historical variable. Instead we have moved from a narrow to a broad view of institutions and from a theoretical proposition to a methodological principle. It is this latter approach that allows for an always embedded economy and the notions of livelihood and the substantive meaning of "economic."

Gemici's argument against the first approach is that Polanyi helps to create the very thing he is arguing against. By conceiving an economic sphere as separate from society he reifies the market economy along what Block and Somers would call market fundamentalist lines. Secondly, his first use of the term is contradicted by his second use of the term. If economic life is an instituted process and always embedded in social life, then it cannot exist as a separate sphere devoid of social content:

> Any recourse into conceiving of these entities as physical spaces constitutes a form of reification. Strictly speaking, economy and society as bounded ontic entities do not exist. As a result, one cannot be embedded in the other, nor can the embeddedness level change over time. (Gemici 2008: 26)

Gemici actually wants to reject the concept of embeddedness because he finds it so limiting. He uses instead the idea of "enmeshment":

> Under his holistic institutionalism, economy is by definition enmeshed in social relations and institutions. Hence, the demarcation between economy and society is absurd; what changes in history as well as from society to society is how these activities are institutionalized and organized. (Gemici 2008: 23)

However, we still have the need to describe, understand and explain what does change. Clearly institutional arrangements do change over time, and from place to place. What language shall we use to refer to this?

Is it possible to discuss varieties of embeddedness instead of levels of embeddedness? What are the structures of embeddedness? Though others have already made suggestions (Nicole Biggart identifies four types as structural, political, cognitive and cultural embeddedness, building on Zukin & DiMaggio), these have not been developed (or "thickened" to use Block's metaphor) (Krippner, Granovetter & Block 2004: 120). Block's response is that "the economy has to be embedded in law, politics, and morality"

(Krippner, Granovetter & Block 2004: 297). This is also helpful. When E.P. Thompson's English crowds demand that bakers sell them bread at a fixed price (not a market price), they are insisting on the application of law—an old law but a law all the same. When the Hebridean crofters invade the Park Forest, they are protesting against the enclosure of lands and the abrogation of customary law. When statute law or common law changes, it can change the bed in which economic relations are negotiated.

When the Poor Law reform ended the obligation of local landowners to provide for the poor in their parishes, it was a political initiative that created a labour market. When the Bank of England was given responsibility for interest rate policy in 1870, it was a political initiative that helped to create the infrastructure for the market for money. Political initiatives, the creation of regulatory institutions and the creation or dismantling of welfare programs can also change the shape and pattern of economic exchange.

Block touches on the question of moral embeddedness when he makes reference to Durkheim's notion of the "non-contractual bases of contract." Market transactions depend heavily on trust. We assume contracts are entered into in good faith. We assume contracts mean what they say. We assume the existence of a whole layer of moral agreement that will support the contract in question. Sometimes contracts are only drawn up long after the basic agreement has been reached and sealed with a handshake.

Even in the modern corporate world, economic behaviour cannot be explained solely by the interplay of supply and demand, nor even by utilitarian calculus. One also needs to understand the moral norms embedded within specific institutional cultures (Jackall 1988).

Legally Embedded versus Morally Embedded

When legal changes don't have popular legitimacy, we see social protest as a result. In those cases I think it is possible to say that a market has been legally disembedded and re-embedded. However, to the extent that this remains contested, it remains partly disembedded—embedded in law but disembedded from morality. Using the contemporary example with which this chapter began, new copyright legislation gives property rights to music publishers. In an era where file-sharing technology gives computer users with internet access the ability to trade, borrow and share music files, an enormous amount of music is being shared on a noncommercial basis. Copyright holders are trying to assert their legal rights to be compensated for this file sharing. The continuing activity of internet-based file sharing in the face of legal threats indicates that the legitimacy of this extension of property law is being contested on moral grounds. The new technology of the computer and the internet creates the potential to share music in new ways and therefore creates the possibility of a market mechanism that governs this activity. A revised law creates a legal structure in which this market finds a home. The law seeks moral legitimacy in order to be supported in practice. If the moral legitimacy is not achieved, the market is not fully embedded in society. The development of the "open source" movement, which has now extended beyond word processing software to biotechnology,[2] and the development of "creative commons" are two examples of attempts to re-embed the market for intellectual property in an alternative moral framework (Lessig 2009).

Block presents one more contemporary example of how the economy can be partially disembedded: the global financial market (Krippner, Granovetter & Block 2004: 289). International capital mobility has increased enormously over the last twenty-five years. Individual national economies can be harmed terribly by massive and sudden capital outflows, as happened in the Asian crisis of 1987 or in Iceland in 2008. Even though the global market is operating with minimal regulation, much more like the laissez-faire regimes of the nineteenth century, nation-states continue to operate on the basis that they are the agents controlling the national markets for labour, land and money. The conflict between these two operating principles periodically generates crisis, as it has in 2008/09.

As in the case of music file sharing, it is new technology that has created the possibility of new global markets in financial derivatives and foreign exchange. The deregulation of the financial sector (a political initiative of governments, e.g., Thatcher and the Big Bang in London, Clinton in New York) allowed these markets to develop. The massive responses of governments to financial crisis in seizing control of banks (Royal Bank of Scotland), allowing some to fail (Lehman Brothers) and forcing the mergers of others (Merrill Lynch with Bank of America) are an example of the speed with which the double movement can occur. The questions raised about the moral legitimacy of using state money to rescue public shareholder corporations (the criticism takes the form of complaints about "privatized profits and socialized debts") suggests that more new infrastructure will re-embed the global financial market.

There is one other possible example of disembedding that is not covered by Block but requires mentioning. Block describes the economy being embedded in law, politics and morality. He does not mention culture. And yet, Polanyi argues that the social catastrophe he is trying so hard to explain is primarily cultural:

> A social calamity is primarily a cultural not an economic phenomenon that can be measured by income figures or population statistics…. Not economic exploitation, as often assumed, but the disintegration of the cultural environment of the victim is then the

cause of the degradation. The economic process may, naturally, supply the vehicle of the destruction, and almost invariably economic inferiority will make the weaker yield, but the immediate cause of his undoing is not for that reason economic; it lies in the lethal injury to the institutions in which his social existence is embodied. The result is loss of self-respect and standards, whether the unit is a people or a class, whether the process springs from so-called "culture conflict" or from a change in the position of a class within the confines of a society. (Polanyi 1957: 157)

It would take more space than I have here to explore what precisely is meant in this case by "culture." However, it does seem to me that Polanyi opens the door to the possibility that another form of disembeddedness may take place, this one as a result of the cultural injury that can be caused by new economic formations. Previously we described disembedding as a change in relationship between legal regulation, political structure, moral attitude and economic behaviour. Using the example of the poor house in the nineteenth century, or what is known today as the "welfare trap," it may be possible to argue that the culture of certain populations can become so damaged that it can no longer contain the economy or reproduce the socially and morally coherent working populations that a modern market economy requires. In the next chapter we will examine some of the economic forces capable of damaging working-class culture in this way.

Instituted versus Embedded

Michele Cangiani, a sociologist teaching in Italy, argues that we should keep the concept of disembeddness and, in doing so, reminds us of two important Polanyian ideas. The first is the concept of an institution, and the second is the concept of autonomy. Cangiani argues that the disagreements stem from a confusion between the idea of an economy being instituted and an economy being embedded. An economy is always instituted because it requires institutions. Even the market is an institution. However, an economy can still be disembedded, even if it is instituted (in the market), because it has become autonomous from the society yet controls humanity and nature and is therefore dominant (Cangiani 2008). It can also still be partially disembedded in the ways I already mentioned—embedded in law and politics but not embedded morally, even though it remains instituted in its market form.

In the end I think embeddedness in institutions is the same thing as being "instituted." The concept depends on the existence of institutions and institutions imply regulations, either formal or informal. However, I also think embeddness in society refers to a relationship of dominance or subordination. So, an economy embedded in feudal society is an economy subordinated to the feudal assumptions of status relationships. But an economy disembedded from society, like market economy, is an economy in a dominant relation to society. So in this way market society is embedded in market economy, not because it is instituted in market economy, but because in market society social relationships are subordinate to economic relationships. In this way as well, the economy seems autonomous from society. However, the relationships are not static but dynamic, and society can be more or less subordinated to market economy and market economy can be more or less disembedded.

We can accept that economic relationships are always embedded in institutions and social relationships, as the sociologists insist. This is a development of Polanyi's thought and requires us to reinterpret the concept of a market society. A market society refers not simply to market economy disembedded from society as two separate spheres, but rather to a society where the economy is organized according to market principles and where the dominant institution in that society is the market—where society is subordinate to the market at the level of ideas. We can also agree that the economy has to be embedded in law, politics and morality (and possibly culture) with the understanding that the economy can be more or less embedded—in a variety of ways, as we have seen, more or less regulated. The concept of embeddedness may still be developed further, but we have not abandoned the concept of disembeddedness and we can still account for the real experiences of social devastation and cultural catastrophe that Polanyi was at pains to explain. It also means the concept of a double movement remains credible as an explanation of social protest and grievance.

Moral Economy as a Discipline of Inquiry

As I indicated at the beginning of the chapter, some scholars have taken the language of moral economy in a new direction, conceiving of it as a discipline of inquiry. One of these is William Booth. A political scientist and a classicist, his specialty is Aristotle. He is a critic of those he calls "moral economists," and yet there is something about the debate he finds helpful. He sees the distinction between an embedded and a disembedded economy as the core concept being advanced. "An embedded economy is one in which the securing of human livelihood is submerged in and determined by a nexus of noneconomic institutions: kinship, citizenship, hierarchy, and so forth" (Booth 1993: 951).

His particular interest stems from his observation that the claim of a normative thrust to economic life has its roots in Aristotelian political philosophy and that "the moral economic approach attempts to restore the question of the telos, of the good to be served by the economy—in a phrase, of its moral embeddedness" (Booth 1993: 953).

Booth's analysis is trenchant but in his interpretation of Polanyi he makes two errors that interfere with the effectiveness of his argument. The first error is that he understands Polanyi to say that scarcity and economizing behaviour are not present in nonmarket economies (Booth 1993: 952, 1994: 659). Actually, Polanyi argues that those societies were not organized around scarcity as the central principle and that economizing action was always present in these earlier societies. This error is a problem because for Booth, the evidence of economizing behaviour in nonmarket or premodern societies is taken as evidence of the weakness of Polanyi's theory.

The second error has to do with his understanding of what the Great Transformation actually refers to. Booth understands the Great Transformation to be the transition from a premodern society, in which economic transactions were embedded in social relationships based on status, to a modern society where the economy had become autonomous (disembedded), society was determined by the rules of the market and relationships were governed by contracts (Booth 1994: 661). As I have written in an earlier chapter, the Great Transformation does not actually refer to the collapse of the old order but rather to the protective response of society and the invention of new mechanisms to re-embed the economy. The confusion occurs because the phrase "The Great Transformation" was not Polanyi's choice for his book, rather it was the choice of his publisher; the phrase has received much more prominence than it would have if the book had been published under Polanyi's proposed title: The Political and Economic Origins of Our Time (see Rotstein 1990: 100). The consequence of these errors is that Booth makes no mention of Polanyi's "double movement." I will show that if he had, it would have strengthened his argument.

Booth joins those other critics who reject the notion of the disembedded economy. Though he does not use this exact phrase, he thinks all economies are embedded. In his analysis of the premodern and embedded economy of ancient Greece, Booth challenges the lack of specificity in identifying how the economy there was actually embedded:

> By leaving unsaid how the economy was subordinated and contained, this approach also causes us to miss something crucial about the theory of market society, namely the extent to which it too is a moral economics, developed in response to the embedded premodern household model.

For Booth, the economy is always embedded in society in two ways, institutionally and normatively. "The institutional context... consists, among other things, of a mesh of property rights made operative in the form of law, of contracts and their enforcement and so on" (Booth 1994: 661).

As a classicist and Aristotelian, Booth is most interested in the normative embedding. He recognizes that, for the moral economist, market society is a contested form that was challenged politically from its beginning, and he welcomes efforts "to keep alive the memory of an economic order different from our own" (Booth 1994: 658). However, he wants to hold up the moral advances made by a society governed by contract rather than status. He demands some recognition that premodern societies were hierarchical, patriarchal and unfree. So for him, the transition from a premodern society to a market society was not a transition from a moral society to an immoral society, but rather a

> moral redrawing of the community and of the place of the economy within it. What that transition yields is a new form of moral embedded-ness for the economy…. At its foundation, this redrawing involves a shift away from the patriarchal household model, with its hierarchal and unfree core. (Booth 1994: 661)

So, from the perspective of moral embeddedness, what Booth sees is not a moral disembedding and re-embedding but rather "the seeking of a balance among competing goods." He describes this as the workings of a society possessing a plurality of goods. Booth is critical of the distinction between embedded economies and disembedded economies, but at the same time he welcomes the territory that this perspective opens up. It retrieves an approach well established in Aristotelian thought that etymologically links the household with the economy:

> Far from being unserviceable, this approach suggests a powerful (and debatable) way of thinking normatively about the economy…. in linking oikos and oikonomiki, "household" and "economics," it intimates another understanding of the economy as located in the mesh of family (or community) relations and purposes. (Booth 1994: 662)

Booth wants to retain the language of moral economy as a method of inquiry because it fits so well with an Aristotelian approach. While he wants to reject the distinction between embeddedness and disembeddedness, he actually maintains it when he claims, "all economies, including the near-to-pervasive-market economies, are moral economies, embedded in the (ethical) framework of their communities" (Booth 1994: 662). Economic relationships or community values change when they are out of synch with each other, but the economy is always morally embedded. For Booth, the advantage of the moral economy discourse as a mode of inquiry is that it reasserts the ancient teleological question: what is wealth for?

Embedded in Moral Norms

Thomas Clay Arnold wants to use the moral economy concept but with an expanded understanding of it. He enters the discussion from the perspective of political science, like both William Booth and James C. Scott, and criticizes on two grounds what he calls the traditional conception of moral economy. First of all, it "rests too heavily on the distinction between non-market and market-based societies and [secondly, it] reduces to the unduly narrow claim that economic incorporation of a non-market people is the basis for the moral indignation that leads to resistance and rebellion" (Arnold 2001: 85). He understands Polanyi to have introduced a distinction not between embedded and disembedded economies, but between embedded and autonomous economies (Arnold 2001: 86). Following William Booth, Arnold argues that market society is normatively embedded (Arnold 2001: 88n4).

Because Arnold wants to use a more robust notion of moral economy, he resists the tendency to restrict its use to instances of rebellion by nonmarket societies against the expansion of market systems. He wants to be able to include in his analysis Meredith Ramsay's account of the crisis in agriculture in Princess Anne County and the crisis in commercial fishing and seafood packing in Crisfield County (Ramsay 1996). She tells the story of these two contemporary Maryland communities resisting commercial real-estate projects, in spite of broad economic decline, because of a near-universal commitment to a shared way of life (Arnold 2001: 88).

He also points to John Walton's study of the Owens Valley in California. Walton describes the violent resistance of people to the expropriation by Los Angeles of valley water. The confrontation started in about 1904, turned violent in 1924, when certain water diversion structures were bombed, and continued into the 1970s, when new environmental laws channeled the conflict into the court system. For Arnold, both of these case studies represent normative conflict over how economic affairs should be organized, even though they don't involve rebellion by subsistence farmers against encroachment by market forces.

> Given its emphasis on the distinction between pre-market and market societies, the prevailing conception of moral economy in political science cannot explain the nonrebellious moral economies of market-structured communities in Maryland, which had achieved a degree of economic development but were reluctant to develop further, even in the face of economic decline. Given its emphasis on resistance to commercial incorporation the prevailing conception of moral economy cannot explain the moral indignation and rebellion of a nonmarket valley in California desperate for commercial incorporation. (Arnold 2001: 89–90)

Arnold's strategy for expanding the moral economy concept is to focus attention on the specific moral norms that legitimate or support resistance to any given economic formation or development. Following Michael Walzer (1983), he encourages us to focus our attention on "social goods [that] harbor the principles communities canvass when judging whether specific developments are legitimate." He understands goods to be

> objects and qualities whose possession or consumption confers some kind of benefit and satisfies human needs and wants.... Even goods considered pure commodities are social, for they consist of shared understandings about the beneficial characteristics attributed to a given object. Any identification of an object as a good unavoidably draws on culturally constructed and culturally transmitted ideas about human needs, wants, and benefits.... Like the meaning of words, the value and meaningfulness of goods are socially determined. (Arnold 2001: 90)

His most vivid example of a social good, loaded with meaning, is short-grain rice in Japan. The Japanese fiercely protect their domestic rice growers even though they could import California-grown rice, grown from the same Japanese root stock, much more cheaply (Arnold 2001: 91).

Arnold advances his social goods approach for three reasons. Firstly, it is not tied to time or culture. It could be applied to any historical period and any culture. Secondly, it allows for multiple social goods and multiple moral economies. Thirdly, it effectively responds to Granovetter's concern about oversocialized conceptions of economic behaviour (Arnold 2001: 94).

All Economies Can Be Examined as Moral Economies

Andrew Sayer is a sociologist teaching at Lancaster University. He is a proponent of the moral economy as a discipline of inquiry rather than an evaluative judgement about any particular form of economic arrangement:

> As a kind of inquiry, "moral economy" is the study of how economic activities of all kinds are influenced and structured by moral dispositions and norms, and how in turn those norms may be compromised, overridden or reinforced by economic pressures. On this definition *all* economies—not merely pre- or non-capitalist ones—are moral economies. We can also use the term "moral economy" to refer to the object of this kind of inquiry. (Sayer 2006: 78)

Sayer values Polanyi's articulation of the "double movement," but he also thinks that the concepts of an embedded and a disembedded economy have certain limitations. In particular, he thinks the metaphor can allow people to overlook the ways in which economic processes are internally influenced; that is, the moral sentiments and decisions of economic actors can influence ongoing economic relationships (Sayer 2004: 2). Sayer has an ongoing research interest in employment relationships. So, it is not surprising that he chooses to focus on the interactive relationship between the moral norms people bring to their workplaces and the ways in which workplace cultures shape the behaviour of individuals who inhabit them. Echoing the work of Clifford Geertz, Sayers describes these economic relationships as "thick," meaning they are characterized by an "ethical surplus" (Sayer 2004: 10). Workers are expected to behave honestly and, in many jobs, are required to cooperate with due regard for the well-being of others. Over time they share experiences and develop shared identities. The giving and receiving of gifts, characteristic of cooperative relationships, thicken the relationships. The tumbling reciprocity binds the individual to the group, and the loss of these relationships can trigger a response similar to bereavement.

It is this account of the thickness of economic relationships and the moral dimension of social life that Sayer finds missing from Polanyi's account and which limits Polanyi's usefulness for understanding moral economy (Sayer 2004: 12). But this is only to say that Sayer and Polanyi do not have identical purposes. Polanyi draws attention to the ethical dimension of economic life and engages in an ethical critique of certain economic arrangements. Sayer wants to show how economic activities of all kinds are influenced and structured by moral dispositions and norms and how in turn those norms may be compromised, overridden or reinforced by economic pressures.

Sayer agrees with Block that "Polanyi's account is far from unitary and not surprisingly is open to many interpretations" (Sayer 2004: 4). He acknowledges that the concept of "disembeddedness" seems like a useful way of describing the shift of commodity production away from need and toward profit. On the other hand, he also wants to claim that all economic processes must be "embedded" in some way. He resolves this tension in the following way:

> There is no contradiction between arguing that capitalist economic processes can be disembedded from, for example, kinship relations or ethnic identities, and yet, as the regulation school has established, rely completely on a social mode of regulation embracing social processes that "stabilize modes of economic calculation and norms of economic conduct" or which run the society "as an adjunct of the market," as Polanyi put it. (Sayer 2006: 81)

This is not very elegantly put and maybe even wrongly put. Polanyi's argument was that "instead of the economic system being embedded in so-cial relationships, these relationships were now embedded in the economic system" (Polanyi 1947: 114). As Polanyi made clear in his *Commentary* article, the mechanism of disembedding was the creation of "fictitious commodities," namely labour, land and money, and the organization of those along market principles. The markets for these commodities were then linked together to form a market system.

Interestingly, Sayer never uses the term "market system," instead choos-ing the term "market" or "market forces." This may be because he prefers the language of capitalism to the language of markets. From his point of view, when "market" is used as a euphemism for capitalism, it "always results in the marginalization and misrepresentation of economic activities not involv-ing market exchange" (Sayer 2006: 78). It would be a major error to think that Polanyi was using the term "market" as a euphemism for "capitalism." On the contrary, he acknowledges the antiquity of markets and even of economizing behaviour. Polanyi analyzes assumptions behind the market system because some of these are shared by Marxists and liberal capitalists alike (Polanyi 1947).

The triumph of the market system is made possible by the political ideology of classical liberalism, also known as laissez-faire. Its triumphant re-emergence in the late twentieth century was made possible by the political ideology of neoliberalism. In this sense one can say that all economies are embedded, because they are shaped and made possible by different forms of political regulation (Ruggie 1982). At this point, it is possible to agree again with Sayer: "The state is involved on both sides, that is both in supporting the establishment of self-regulating markets, and as one of the actors defending society against their negative effects" (Sayer 2006: 82). While it is true that political regulation may be imposed upon markets by external authorities, it is also true that moral regulations suffuse those same markets and also form a part of their preconditions.

The Economy Is Always Embedded in Society

We have learned from Polanyi and Thompson to interpret the appearance of a protest-based moral economy as the back half of the double movement—of social self-protection against the corrosive effects of the utopian, supposedly self-regulating, market system. We have also seen that some have now taken this style of analysis in a new direction. Rather than restricting the concept of a moral economy to an ideal state of affairs (Powleson 1998) or to moments of social protest, these thinkers conceive of the moral economy as a discipline of inquiry. This shift is based on the idea that the economy is *always embedded* in society, and therefore the moral character of economic relationships is always available for scrutiny. This represents a serious challenge to Polanyi's analysis. Does the presumption of an *always embedded economy* mean that the concept of the double movement is no longer credible?

Our answer is no. However, we have identified the need to flesh out the different meanings of embeddedness. We agree with Polanyi and Cangiani that the economy is an instituted process. All economies require institutions for their expression, even if the institution is the market. Institutions imply regulation whether the regulations are formal, as in legal and political regulations, or whether they are informal, as in moral and cultural regulation. In this way we agree with Granovetter and Barber that all economies are embedded, meaning all economies require regulation of different kinds. We also agree with Krippner and Block that economies can be partly disembedded from regulatory regimes for limited periods of time.

In a separate meaning of embeddedness, we can also say that, in market society, the economy is disembedded from society because it has shifted from a subordinate to a dominant role in the relationship. The market economy can never become truly autonomous from society. However, because land, labour and money are now organized according to market principles, society is now subordinate to the market at the level of ideas.

Finally, because the economy is always embedded morally, it is possible to conceive of moral economy as a discipline of inquiry as well as a state of affairs. Any economic activity may be embedded in a moral system that we either currently support (voluntary blood donation) or find morally repugnant (slave labour), but the substantive economy remains embedded. However, where the market economy continues to expand we may find circumstances in which a market is partially embedded in law and politics but at the same time contested and therefore partially disembedded in morality and culture.

Back to Downloaded Music

The market for property rights in digital music is embedded in American law through the Digital Theft Deterrence Act. However, it is not embedded in morality or culture. Not only are there professors and academic institutes that think digital file sharing is not theft, there are artists who also share this view. John Perry Barlow, lyricist for the musical group the Grateful Dead, believes that the online world presents us with a new form of the "gift economy," "where no moral blameworthiness attaches to non-commercial sharing."[3] When new markets are created, morality is often contested. When public libraries were created, large publishers campaigned against them because borrowing books was going to take away from their profits. It is still possible to find old paperbacks with a notice inside the front cover warning the reader that the book could not be lent or even resold.

Markets require legitimacy—political, legal and moral legitimacy. When Mahatma Gandhi marched his followers to the sea in order to make their own salt, he was breaking the British law by refusing to pay the salt tax. Was he a criminal? According to the British colonial legal system, yes. Was he morally right? According to the Indian people, yes, even more so.

Notes

1. You can follow Joel's story at <http://joelfightsback.com>.
2. The Cambia BIOS Initiative promotes Biological Innovation for Open Society. It is an organization based in Australia dedicated to the creation of biotechnologies which can be shared in an open source approach to achieve transparency and accessibility. It was created by Dr. Richard Jefferson, who conducted the first field release of a transgenic food crop. See <www.bios.net>.
3. See Affadavit signed by John Perry Barlow, 1 April 2009, "Sony BMG Music Entertainment et al. v. Joel Tenenbaum, United States District Court, Massachusetts" Docket # 07-CV-11446-NG; available at <http://joelfightsback.com/about-the-case/legal-documents/>.

5. Marginalization and the Shadow Side of Economic Globalization

Marginalization: The Problem of Centres

In 1903 John Caird, Master of Oxford's Balliol College, challenged three bright young students to "go to the East End of London and find out what poverty is, and why in Britain there is so much grinding poverty alongside great wealth, and work out what can be done about it." One of those students was R.H. Tawney, who went on to become one of the greatest historians of his generation. Tawney's answer to Caird's question can be found in his advice to the next generation of students: "start much higher up the stream than the point [you] wish to reach... what thoughtful rich people call the problem of poverty, thoughtful poor people call with equal justice the problem of riches" (Tawney 1983: 48). With parallel logic we can say that marginalization is in fact a problem of centres.

It has become common today to refer to those without sufficient income or resources as the "marginalized." One hundred years ago academics would have referred to this same group of people as the "poor." The shift from the language of poverty to the language of marginalization is in part an attempt to broaden the category beyond the purely economic. In spite of the reams of economic data that are still conventionally used—gross national product (GNP), unemployment rates and the like—there is a desire to take into account other forms of social injustice like racial, gender and ethnic oppression. Rarely do we spend time reflecting on the root concept of the "margin."

Consider the following:

What is this? The simple answer is: it is a line on the page. A line can divide but it cannot contain. One can be on one side of the line, or on the other side, but you can't be inside it or outside it. A single line is not a margin. However, when I add some more lines, it becomes something different.

Now, with three additional lines, I have created a box. It now has spaces defined as *inside* and *outside*. These lines have now defined *margins*. Inside the box, the closer you are to the line, the closer you are to the margin. The farther away you are from the lines, the closer you are to the centre. Margins require boundaries. Boundaries exist for the purpose of *exclusion*. If you are being pushed away from the centre, you are traveling toward the margin and if you pass the margin, you will be excluded altogether.

If the rectangle drawn above is a metaphor for society (it could be a circle just as well as a square), you can see that what we are talking about is *social exclusion*. Marginalization, then, has to do with power, with participation in decision making and with belonging. Margins require centres and marginalization is a matter of relationship. As the philosopher John Macmurray articulated, to be a person is to be in relationship (Macmurray 1961). The first experience of an infant child is the relationship with its mother. Before there is a me, there is a we. Persons are by nature social beings, and so the process of social exclusion is also a process whereby we render some to be nonpersons.

The process of social exclusion, of marginalization, has taken on some new characteristics in the last forty years. The period from the end of World War II until the mid 1970s saw an increase in industrialization in the West. This led to greater wealth generally and to an expansion of that group of workers who were wealthy enough to own their own homes, commonly called the "middle class." The rise in home ownership is sometimes taken as analogous to increasing equality. It is such a powerful analogy that it became a matter of U.S. public policy in the 1990s to encourage the extension of mortgages to unqualified borrowers, otherwise known as "subprime borrowers." However, over the last thirty-five years there has been an increase in social inequality even as home ownership rates have increased or stayed the same.[1] We have seen an increase in indebtedness, an increase in very high incomes, an increase in poverty and a shrinking of the number of middle-income earners. In the first half of the twentieth century there were dramatic declines in the share of national income earned by the richest in various countries. However, in the last two or three decades of that century, there was an almost complete recovery of income share by the wealthiest in the United States (Piketty and Saez 2003), a partial recovery by them in the United Kingdom (Atkinson 2002) and no recovery at all in France (Piketty 2003). In Great Britain in 1976 the top 10 percent of the population had incomes 2.9 times greater than the bottom 10 percent. Twenty-five years later the ratio had risen to 4:1 (Sayer 2005: 230). Some call this the hollowing out of Western societies and attribute it to the loss of well-paid manufacturing jobs as factories closed and were moved to low-wage countries.[2] It may also be possible that this is more a symptom than a cause if the change can be attributed to more fundamental shifts in socio-economic arrangements. What we do know is that income inequality in the United States is the highest of all the developed countries, and has increased for families by over 23 percent between 1968 and 1994. By the middle of the last decade, the top 20 percent of income earners earned almost half the total national income, which was thirteen times the share of the poorest 20 percent (Hicks 2000: 5).

Income distribution is less unequal in Canada but the trends are the same. Between 1976 and 2004 the poorest 20 percent of Canada's families saw their share of national earnings fall from 4.5 to 2.6 percent. In the same period the richest 10 percent of families saw their share of total earnings grow from 73 to 79.5 percent. In 2004 the average earnings of the richest 10 percent of Canada's families raising children was eighty-two times that earned by the poorest 10 percent of Canada's families. This is almost three times the ratio of 1976, when it was approximately 31:1 (Yalnizian 2007).

> [Since 1985] top income shares in Canada have increased dra-matically, almost as much as in the United States. This change has remained largely unnoticed because it is concentrated within the top percentile of the Canadian income distribution.... As in the United States, the increase is largely due to a surge in top wages and salaries. (Saez and Veall 2005: 832)

A recent report shows what marginalization looks like in my home town of Toronto (Toronto Community Foundation 2009). Toronto is the largest city in Canada with a population in the Census Metropolitan Area (CMA) of 5.5 million. According to the international human resources firm Mercer, in 2009 Toronto ranked 15th out of 215 cities around the world for its quality of life. It is the second wealthiest city in Canada (after Vancouver), with an average household net worth of $562,000. However, Toronto is also a very expensive place to live. The average cost of basic nutritious food for a family

"Since 1998 Canada's top 100 CEOs saw a 262% increase in compensation, pocketing an average of $9.1 million in 2005 compared to $3.5 million in 1998. Meanwhile, the average Canadian worker made just over $38,000 in a year, a 15% increase over the average earnings of 1998 (just over $33,000). CPI increased by 17.85% in that same period meaning that, after adjusting earnings for inflation, the average worker actually lost purchasing power."
—Yalnizian 2007

of four rose 9.4 percent over the last two years. A family of four would need to spend more than is provided by social assistance just for food and housing (33 percent of its income on food and 72 percent on rent). More than 30 percent of Toronto children under the age of five are in families below the low income cut-off, a figure commonly used to identify the poverty line. For our purposes, what is significant is not the current state of crisis affecting poor families but rather the change in their circumstances over the last thirty or forty years. For example, in 1979, 66 percent of Toronto neighbourhoods were middle-income, meaning the average individual income was within 20 percent (above or below) of the average for the CMA. By 2005 that number had fallen to just 29 percent of neighbourhoods. Researchers expect that only 20 percent of Toronto's neighbourhoods will be middle-income by 2025 if current trends continue. Families in the top 10 percent of income earners in the region earn 10.6 times the income of families in the bottom 10 percent.

The Moral Economy of Class

"Having once been the fundamental source and subject of conflict in the political culture of capitalism, class inequality is now the problem that dare not speak its name." — Sayer 2005: 224.

In North America especially, the category of analysis known as "class" is almost entirely absent from social and political discourse. This is partly because the social conflict over class was something European immigrants left behind in the Old World. Partly it is because the collapse of the Soviet Union in 1991 removed the need for Western politicians to respond to the challenges of Marxist categories. Partly it is because Western ideology reinterpreted the category of class in a way that deviates from the Marxist understanding of proximity to the ownership of the means of production and control over the labour of others, turning instead toward income levels, educational achievement and employment status. In the United States and Canada, in popular discourse the middle class is thought to be the largest group in society even though in other countries people doing the same work would be considered working class (Thompson and Hickey 2005; Ehrenreich 1989). For example, in Canada, a unionized janitor and a teacher, both working for a public school board, would be considered middle class, though some might use education or professional status to distinguish between upper- and lower-middle class.

In the absence of a sustained public debate about class, the push for equality has focused on gender and race. For example, since the Canadian constitution was amended in 1982 to include the Charter of Rights, it has

"Though an ideal of an equal distribution of material wealth may continue to elude us, it is necessary, nevertheless, to make haste towards it, not because such wealth is the most important of man's treasures, but to prove that it is not." — Tawney 1931: 291

been illegal in Canada to discriminate on the basis of race, national or ethnic origin, colour, religion, sex, age or mental or physical disability. Nowhere is the category of income or socio-economic status recognized as a prohibited ground of discrimination. Economic inequality is not merely a category of discrimination that can be added to other forms of discrimination. It is a category produced by the structure of capitalism, and it can also be reproduced in many ways. It can be reproduced by language and culture, as is so obvious in the United Kingdom. It can be reproduced by education, as is obvious in France and the United States. As Andrew Sayer puts it, "Class is therefore both 'structural' to capitalism, yet contingently co-determined by many non-capitalist influences" (Sayer 2005: 224).

If the concept of a moral economy can be understood not only as a state of affairs but also as a discipline of inquiry, then a moral economy approach will be concerned with how economic arrangements affect conditions of economic inequality. "Class matters because it creates unequal possibilities for flourishing and suffering" (Sayer 2005: 218). A moral economy approach will listen for voices protesting over issues of both sufficiency and equity. Concern for sufficiency is a concern about not having enough to eat or enough resources to participate meaningfully in social life—the contemporary definition of poverty. If you can't participate meaningfully you are being pushed to the margins of society. Concern for equity is a concern for fairness in the distribution of resources. Those resources include income, wealth and respect. In the negative form they also include contempt, envy, resentment or condescension and deference. This is one of the reasons why some people argue that "the major systems of oppression are interlocking" (see Combahee River Collective Statement 1977, in Marable and Mullings 2000). North Americans have relied on a rapidly expanding economy to blunt the negative impacts of class formation. As long as the class of middle-income earners continues to grow, conflicts over the distribution of resources can be ameliorated. However, if that situation changes, as it appears to have done, we can expect issues of wealth distribution and class to come back strongly onto the public agenda.

Observing these dramatic trends, one might ask: what has changed in the last thirty to forty years? It may well be that this question will be easier to answer in another fifty years' time. Some truly significant events have happened in this period. One of the most dramatic was the fall of the Berlin Wall in 1989. This signaled the release of the U.S.S.R.'s stranglehold on the countries of Eastern Europe and the end of the Cold War. The U.S.S.R.

itself collapsed in 1991. This might have meant a major shift of economic resources away from military expenditure, and there was certainly discussion of the possibility of a "peace dividend," but the U.S. invasion of Iraq in the first Gulf War (1990/91) provided a new rationale for re-armament. Another major event was the 2001 hijacking of commercial airliners and bombing of New York's World Trade Center and the Pentagon, in what is now referred to as "9/11." This presented another justification for renewed U.S.-led invasions of Afganistan and Iraq. As dramatic and significant as these events are, they don't explain a forty-year increase in social inequality and a corresponding rise in class antagonism.

Economic Globalization

The one event that does explain this change is the process that now goes by the term "economic globalization." The word globalization is something of a chimera. It seems to mean whatever anyone wants it to mean. In cultural terms it is used to refer to a common Western-style culture where people listen to the same music wherever they live; or to a common cultural experience in which people in Thailand become fans of the Manchester United football club, or people in China become fans of the Houston Rockets basketball team. In religion, globalization sometimes refers to an increase in interfaith dialogue or an increase in awareness of the diversity of contemporary religious experience and expression. In the context of communications, globalization refers to the ease with which people can now communicate with each other across the globe, especially by virtue of the internet.

The diversity of definitions is now so great that we find some writers becoming quite philosophical about it. Regarding globalization and health, Dr. Kelley Lee, former chair of the World Health Organization's Scientific Resource Group on Globalization, Trade and Health, defines globalization in terms of three types of changes: spatial, temporal and cognitive (Lee 2004). Spatial changes have to do with the increase in movement of people, information, goods and services across national borders in such a way that it challenges the capacity of national governments to regulate it. Temporal changes have to do with how communication and transportation technologies speed up our lives and increase the pressure to multitask, even while the same processes lead to gridlocked roads and information overload. Cognitive changes have to do with how our cultures are being changed and with them our perceived wants, needs, desires and values (Lee 2004: 2).

Here, I will define globalization in more narrowly economic terms. Even here, though, there is great difference of opinion. For many people in business and politics, economic globalization refers to an increase in world trade. According to standard economics, when two parties trade from their surplus, both parties are better off. How could an increase in trade be anything other than a good thing? This is surely what the former President of Mexico Ernesto Zedillo meant when he wrote: "Globalization has, in short, been an incredible force for good in the world." For him, "The new players [like China] have made world trade more dynamic and enlarged the pool of world savings available to finance the substantial current account deficits incurred by the U.S. in recent years" (Zedillo 2006).

For other business leaders, globalization refers to increased freedom for corporations and other investors of capital and decreased regulation by the state. Consider the following definition offered at the World Economic Forum in Davos, Switzerland, by the president of the transnational electronics and power supply company ABB:

> I would define globalization as the freedom of my group of compa-
> nies to invest where it wants, when it wants, to produce what it wants,
> to buy and sell where it wants, and support the fewest restrictions
> possible coming from labour laws and social conventions. (*Le Devoir*,
> 30 November 1999, quoted by Beaudin & Coté 2002)

This definition of globalization emphasizes the changing relationship between all large companies as a class and all governments as a whole. Some people call it corporate globalization, and it doesn't distinguish between the companies of one nation and the companies of another. In contrast, consider the definition offered by former U.S. Secretary of State Henry Kissinger during a lecture at Trinity College Dublin in 1999:

> The basic challenge is that what is called globalization is really an-
> other name for the dominant role of the United States. (Kissinger
> 1999)

This definition is more political than economic and slides into a synonym for imperialism. Many people use the term in this way, and this may be even more common on the political left than on the political right. For example, Sam Gindin, former CAW economist, describes globalization as capitalism writ large. It has already had several lives and can be part of the imperial project of whatever nation currently hoists the capitalist flag. In the nineteenth century it was Great Britain, and in the twentieth century it was the United States. He writes:

> The U.S. state, with its overwhelming postwar resources and power,
> consciously shaped that globalization. It didn't follow market pres-
> sures, but *led* them. Determined to avoid the disaster of the previous
> era of globalization and its threat to capitalism itself, the U.S. state set
> out to minimize the opposition between national and international
> economies. The goal was to rebuild devastated national economies

while also integrating them into global networks. The U.S.-led internationalization of economic, political, and military ties didn't weaken national states but, by supporting growth and weakening domestic opposition, it actually strengthened the national status quo and the national state. (Gindon 2002)

In the same vein, Dani Rodik, professor of international political economy at Harvard's Kennedy School of Government, writes, "The world economy has seen globalization collapse once already. The gold standard era—with its free capital mobility and open trade—came to an abrupt end in 1914 and could not be resuscitated after World War I" (Rodik 2008). This definition of globalization as imperialism follows from Marx's analysis in the Communist Manifesto of the expansionary tendencies within capitalism.

A century and a half ago, Karl Marx noted capitalism's inherent drive to "nestle everywhere, settle everywhere, establish connections everywhere.... In place of the old national seclusion and self-sufficiency, we have intercourse in every direction, the universal interdependence of nations" (Marx 1979 [1848]: 476).

The definition of globalization as imperialism is a compelling one if for no other reason than because the core image of the globe suggests that connection. The first terrestrial globes to survive date from the end of the fifteenth century and the beginning of the sixteenth century, the early days of European imperialism in the so-called New World. Today the most popular image associated with globalization is a photograph of the Earth as seen from the moon. The first such photo was taken in 1966. The first landing on the moon by a person was in 1969. In both cases these were U.S. achievements and were seen as markers of U.S. imperial supremacy. However, this is not the definition I am using here. This does not mean imperialism doesn't exist. It does. But I am trying to get behind the specific imperialism of today to analyze the context in which imperialism takes place. The British empire supplanted the Spanish empire and was succeeded in turn by the U.S. empire. Today we are living through the death throes of the U.S. empire. (Just because it is dying doesn't make it less dangerous.) We may also be witnessing the beginning of a new Chinese empire, if the rush by China to acquire Africa's mineral resources is any indication. But what is shaping the context in which these imperialist struggles are waged? The context is being determined by a revolution in the relationship between the economy and society, caused by the linking together of national markets to form a single global market. That is why I define economic globalization as "the process of creating integrated global markets for goods, services, capital and labour, and the social effects of this process."

I have described the process of economic globalization as a revolution

Table 5.1 The Revolution Called Globalization

ECONOMY	TECHNOLOGY	SOURCE OF WEALTH
Agricultural	Plough	Land
	Industrial Revolution	
Industrial	Steam Engine	Factory
	Global Revolution	
Knowledge	Computer Chip	Intellectual Property

for two reasons. The first is that a revolution turns everything upside down, and globalization has done that for us, specifically in terms of the relationship between the economy and society. Instead of society determining the goals of justice that an efficient economy might achieve, now we find economic agents (business leaders, political leaders) telling society how it should reorganize itself in order to become more efficiently competitive. Justice is paid for with what's left over.

The second reason I describe the process of economic globalization as a revolution is to evoke the cultural memory of the last major social and economic revolution—the Industrial Revolution. This revolution occurred first in the United Kingdom in the late eighteenth century[3] and subsequently spread to Europe, the Americas and the rest of the world. It dominated the U.K. in the nineteenth century because it was experienced as both sudden and also overwhelming, but in the rest of the world it is described as a process of industrialization because it happened more slowly and was recognizable.

The Industrial Revolution[4] marked the shift from an agricultural economy to an industrial economy. The key technology in an agricultural economy was the plough. Improvements to this technology (from the scratch plough to the wooden mouldboard plough to the iron and steel mouldboard ploughs, for example) greatly increased productivity and generated more wealth. This wealth accrued not to the labourer who tilled the field but to the owner of the land.

In an industrial economy, agriculture is still important, but it is no longer the dominant economic activity. In Britain in the nineteenth century, the key technology was the steam engine. It was first used to pump water out of mines, greatly increasing the productivity of mining. However, its most significant impact was in the textile industry. A steam engine could be placed inside a building and used to drive power looms, the first of which was patented in 1785. This greatly increased the productivity of the textile industry, and the buildings where these manufactures took place (to manufacture originally meant to make by hand) became known as factories. The wealth generated by these factories again accrued not to the labourers but not to the owners of land either. This time it went to the owners of the factories. The only owners of land who continued to prosper in this new economy were those landowners who discovered they could strip off the topsoil and mine the coal underneath. It was coal that powered the steam engines, and there was a large and growing demand for it.

Steam engines could also be placed on boats, and so steamboats were invented, improving the reliability of water transportation, which was no longer dependent on the wind.[5] Steam engines were then put on iron rails, and the locomotive was invented, transforming the early horse-drawn railways. Steam-powered railroads transformed the transportation of goods and people in the nineteenth century. Arguably it made the Canadian nation-state possible. So, these are some of the reasons why I say that the steam engine was the key technology of the new industrial economy.

We are now living through another revolution, just as profound as the Industrial Revolution. We call this one the revolution of globalization. In this revolution we are experiencing the transition from the industrial economy to the knowledge-based economy. The key technology in this revolution is the computer chip.[6] This is the popular name for an integrated circuit, first successfully demonstrated by Jack Kilby of Texas Instruments in 1958.[7] These computer chips were essential to the success of the Apollo space program, and now they are everywhere. They serve as the foundation for all computers, cellular phones, MP3 players and digital appliances. Even my toaster has one. More significantly, in addition to its uses for communication, it is now foundational to modern manufacturing, mining and transportation—just like the steam engine in its time.

The wealth generated by the computer chip does not accrue to the workers assembling them in ultra-clean factories; it doesn't even accrue to the owners of the factories, at least not in any new way. In the new knowledge-based economy, the wealth generated by this technology accrues to the owners of intellectual property. Intellectual property refers to a temporary legal monopoly granted to owners of patents, copyright, trademarks and the like. They represent a property right in the form of an idea, an invention or a sign used in business. The ubiquitous Microsoft Corporation has approximately $60 billion in annual sales. The property it owns is primarily intellectual property. The cost of a computer disk itself is only a tiny fraction of the cost of the software instructions encoded on the disk and, increasingly, the physical disk is disappearing from the transaction altogether. A company whose wealth is generated by intellectual property no longer needs to own actual factories. It can simply license another party to manufacture its product. The license is a temporary right to use the intellectual property for this purpose.

Financial Globalization

The driver behind this revolution called globalization is a change in world-wide financial markets, and that is why economic globalization is sometimes referred to as financial globalization. I have told some of this story in an earlier book (Lind 1995a), so let me recap it here before updating it. After World War II, the international trading system needed to be rebuilt. The United States was the largest industrialized country that had not been devastated by the war. It was also owed large amounts of money which had been lent to its allies to fund the war effort. So, the United States had all the money and most of the undamaged industrial capacity. In 1944 a conference was held in Bretton Woods, New Hampshire, for the allied powers to plan the reconstruction of the international economic system. The two most prominent economic voices were Britain's John Maynard Keynes and the American Harry Dexter White.

In order for the international trading regime to be re-established, money needed to be redistributed and postwar currencies needed to be stabilized. It was agreed that currencies would have a fixed rate of exchange but these would also be adjustable. Nations would balance their currency surpluses and deficits by exchanging currency with the United States at a value of US$35/ounce of gold. Governments without a large supply of domestic gold to hold in reserve could hold U.S. dollars instead, because it was "as good as gold." The United States had been on the gold standard until 1933, when President Roosevelt changed the law to prevent United States citizens from redeeming their dollars for gold at the bank. At the international level, though, it was still the standard used by national governments to balance their accounts. At this same Bretton Woods conference, two key institutions were created. The International Monetary Fund oversees the global financial system and is concerned especially with currency exchange rates and balance of payments. The International Bank for Reconstruction and Development was focused on rebuilding economies devastated by war. In 1945 it joined with four other international institutions to form the World Bank. Its mission has now expanded to include poverty reduction.

In the 1950s, as trade was being rebuilt and the Korean War was being fought, the U.S. dollar became the *de facto* international currency. It wasn't just the French government using U.S. dollars to balance its account with Brazil. It was also Canadian companies trading with those in Argentina, or Germans trading with Indians, that were using U.S. dollars both as their medium of exchange and their measure of account. During this period there grew a pool of foreign U.S. dollars that never got returned to the United States. They just circulated from one international capital to another as the preferred currency of exchange. The pool of cash became known as the Eurodollar market, and in 1959 it represented about US$1 billion. Transnational corporations

"The first three decades after 1945 were governed by the Bretton Woods consensus—a shallow multilateralism that permitted policymakers to focus on domestic social and employment needs while enabling global trade to recover and flourish. This regime was superseded in the 1980s and 1990s by an agenda of deeper liberalization and economic integration." — Rodik 2008

came to rely on it more and more as an inexpensive source for borrowed money, and it grew very rapidly. As Andrew Kreiger notes, "By 1973 the sum of U.S. dollars sloshing around in the Eurodollar market was about US$80 billion. By 1977 the Eurodollar market would amount to some US$380 billion" (Krieger 1992: 127). By 1987, the Eurocurrency market (which now included new currencies, hence the new name) totaled nearly US$4 trillion (Levitch and Walter 1989: 53).

In the 1960s, while international lending and trade through the Eurodollar market was booming, the United States was rapidly expanding its money supply to pay for the Vietnam War. This created a trade imbalance because the U.S. bought more imported goods than it exported. At the end of 1970, total claims against the U.S. dollar were three times greater than the value of U.S. gold reserves (Krieger 1992: 136). For some time a crisis was averted. The U.S. Federal Reserve put pressure on central banks around the world not to demand gold, and those central banks "did everything possible to avoid buying surplus dollars from the domestic banks" (Bolton 1970: 7). However, in early August 1971, when Britain inquired about redeeming US$3 billion for gold, the crisis arrived. The U.S. realized they had just been asked to hand over a quarter of their gold reserves in a single transaction. On August 15, 1971, President Nixon announced that the U.S. dollar would no longer be convertible to gold. Since that time, in spite of various agreements to manage currency values, most international currencies have had a floating value relative to each other. Those values are now determined in a market created by daily transactions that totaled US$3.2 trillion in 2007 (BIS 2007).

When the gold standard was abandoned, the cartel of oil-producing countries called OPEC (Organization of the Petroleum Exporting Countries) worried that their own assets and income would be severely eroded. Their response was to put the price of oil on a "gold standard." The resultant rapid rise in the price of oil became known as the "oil shock" of 1973.[8] This produced a new inflow of US$150 billion into the economies of those countries *each year*—much more than they were able to absorb. As a solution to this problem, they invested this excess money in U.S. and European banks. All of a sudden, the large international banks had enormous new sources of capital to lend. It was at this time that the commercial lending policies of the banks became very aggressive. This was also the period in which most of the original Third World debt was accumulated. As Adrian Hamilton put it, the financial system could manage

> only because the oil producers, being relatively unsophisticated in finance, preferred to use the banks as the natural channel for their surplus funds. The first result of this "intermediation," as it was called, was the explosion in international banking and syndicated loans (or lending by groups of banks) of the 1970s. The subsequent debt crisis among Third World borrows has been in the headlines ever since. (Hamilton 1986: 22)

The transformation of the international financial system was still only partially understood in the 1970s. The forced recycling of Western consumption dollars into OPEC investment dollars and again into Third World debt dollars might have been positive except for the developments of 1979. In October of that year, Paul Volcker, the head of the U.S. Federal Reserve Board, decided to try to control inflation by restricting the money supply. He did this by raising the cost of money lent to commercial banks—i.e., he raised interest rates for banks who borrowed money from the Reserve. This would have been an unexceptional maneuver had it been done by the Governor of the Bank of Canada, but it was being done by the head of the United States central bank. Though the U.S. was no longer on the gold standard, the U.S. dollar was still the world's currency. Most international trade was still carried on in U.S. dollars. Most foreign governments continued to hold U.S. dollars in reserve to back their own currencies. By raising the central bank rate in the U.S., Paul Volcker was effectively raising the central bank rate for the world. Michael Lewis described it this way:

> On October 6, 1979, Volker announced that the money supply would cease to fluctuate with the business cycle; money supply would be fixed, and interest rates would float... in practice, the shift in the focus of monetary policy meant that interest rates would swing wildly.... Overnight the bond market was transformed from a backwater into a casino. (Lewis 1989, 35)

Eventually, interest rates rose to 22 percent. In August 1982 Mexico stopped making payments on its foreign debt because rising interest rates made it impossible. Mexico's announcement was soon followed by similar ones from Brazil, Venezuela, Argentina and Chile. In that year, outstanding U.S. loans to these five countries were larger than the total capital of the entire banking system of the United States (Frieden 1987: 119). This dramatic change in circumstances was not only a problem in international lending. It affected domestic lending as well. With the need to recirculate petrodollars, bankers not only aggressively pursued loans in developing nations. They also pursued new loans among Canadian farmers. For example, in 1971 farmers in Saskatchewan (Canada's bread basket) paid Cdn$53 million in interest on loans. By 1981, that figure had increased to almost Cdn$450 million, and many bankruptcies ensued (Lind 1995a: 34).

There is another key narrative stemming from Nixon's decision to float the U.S. currency. While today we take for granted that the exchange rate for international currencies will be different from one day to the next, in 1971 that was not the case. Actually, it took most of that decade for the other major industrialized countries to unpeg their own currencies and a full ten years for the world to realize the U.S. no longer had the power to control foreign exchange. However, it was clear to some that one implication of Nixon's decision was that all international trade would now have a significant foreign currency aspect. This realization led to the creation of what we now call the derivatives market.

A derivative is a financial instrument derived from an underlying asset. For example, when a bond is issued (even a government bond) there are two parts to it. There are the annual interest payments, and then there is the repayment of the principal amount. A $1,000 bond issued at 5 percent for ten years will produce $50 a year in interest and a $1,000 payment at the end of ten years. Traditionally, the bond would be printed in the form of a certificate. The main portion of the certificate would represent the principal payment and the annual interest payments would be represented by coupons attached to the main document. The interest portion could be stripped away from the rest of the document and sold separately. How much would you pay today for ten annual payments of $50? The principal payment could also be sold separately. How much would you pay today for a promise to pay you $1,000 in ten years' time? These were called "stripped bonds," and they were an early form of derivative. Another early form was futures contracts.

Futures contracts had become a significant earner on the Chicago Mercantile Exchange (CME) in the early 1960s with the development of the frozen pork belly contract. However, the trade was still primarily in agricultural products and was considered a sleepy business. "By 1968, traders were 'sitting on the steps of the [soy] bean pit… reading newspapers'" (MacKenzie & Millo 2003: 113). In the early 1970s, the CME's Leo Melamed and University of Chicago economist Milton Friedman approached the board of the First National Bank of Chicago with the idea of trading not frozen pork bellies, or even corn, but cash (Diamond & Kollar 1989: 10). What Friedman understood but others did not was that the advent of floating currency exchange rates would introduce a new level of risk into international trade, against which importers and/or exporters would want to buy insurance. For example, a Toyota dealer in Chicago might place an order in

January for delivery in September of a shipment of cars from Japan. The Chicago dealer would have to agree on a price in January without knowing what the dollar/yen exchange rate would be nine months hence. The auto dealer might want to hedge their risk through a contract whereby a third party agrees to supply a sufficient quantity of Japanese yen in nine months' time in return for a certain fee.

This argument was persuasive, and the market for financial futures was born. It grew rapidly. In 1984 the Chicago Mercantile Exchange joined with Singapore to offer twenty-four-hour-a-day trading in financial futures. By 1987 more than 310 million futures contracts were traded throughout the world, and 66 percent were traded in Chicago.[9] By 1992 the foreign exchange market dwarfed the combined operations of the New York, London, Frankfurt and Tokyo stock exchanges (Kreiger 1992: 15). As of September 2009, the Chicago Mercantile Exchange was trading 10.5 million derivatives contracts daily (CME Group Website 2009). As Mackenzie and Millo put it: "In 1970, financial derivatives were unimportant (no reliable figures for market size exist). By June 2000, the total notional amount of derivatives contracts outstanding worldwide was $108 trillion, the equivalent of $18,000 for every human being on earth" (MacKenzie & Millo 2003: 109).

Another form of derivative is known as a "currency swap." Salomon Brothers engineered one of the first currency swaps, between IBM and the World Bank in 1981. IBM needed a large amount of money in U.S. dollars and had excess supplies of Swiss francs and German marks as a result of bond sales in those currencies. The World Bank always needed cash in many currencies. Salomon Brothers arranged for IBM and the World Bank to swap their currencies without selling each other the underlying bonds (Tett 2009: 12). The two organizations swapped their currency risk without selling their obligations. This novel arrangement quickly became common practice across financial capitals.

I have defined economic globalization as *the process of creating integrated global markets for goods, services, capital and labour, and the social effects of this process.* The first truly integrated global market among this group has been the market for financial capital. It was the first because of the impact of computerization. Its increase in size has been so great and so rapid that it has overwhelmed the protective dykes erected by previous generations. This has had the effect of transferring power from political and social institutions to economic ones. This phenomenon is so new that we are still trying to grasp its implications.

I have described how the inflation of the U.S. dollar led eventually to the abandonment of the gold standard, the formation of futures and derivatives markets, the expansion of credit through the recirculation of petrodollars, the era of high interest rates and the debt crisis among less-developed countries.

Throughout the 1980s much political attention was focused on rescheduling foreign debt payments, even though for many of the world's poor the efforts were a day late and a penny short. This stark reality was indicative of deep changes going on in the world's financial foundations. The deputy governor of the Bank of England described the 1980s this way:

> During the last two or three years... international banking—and indeed financial activity more generally—has embarked on changes which are probably as far-reaching as any in its long history.... But these will, I think, be outstripped in the breadth of their impact, both on financial institutions and on the range of instruments available to borrowers and lenders, by what is going on now. (Hamilton 1986: 13)

On October 19, 1987, the world's stock markets crashed. People call it Black Monday because the Dow Jones Industrial Average plunged 22.61 percent in one day. In New Zealand it is called Black Tuesday because of the time zone difference and because the market there ended up falling 60 percent. The significance of this event is that the fall is largely attributed to what is known as "program trading." That is, it was caused by computer programs that were set to sell in response to certain indicators, without factoring in the possibility that most other market participants were also computers. The new technology was showing its shadow side.

During this same period international bankers were starting to realize something new was happening. In 1983 Canada participated in an experimental research project coordinated by the Bank of International Settlements (BIS) in Switzerland. The BIS is a bank for the world's central banks. The project tracked the amount of foreign currency that was exchanged over the course of one month. They repeated the calculations every three years. In April 1983 the equivalent of US$103 billion was exchanged in Canada with 90 percent of that involving transactions with the Canadian and U.S. currencies. Twelve years later, in April 1995, that figure had risen to more than US$580 billion. By comparison, the total value of imports and exports in Canada averages about $40 billion a month and doesn't vary by more than 30 percent over a five-year period. It also means that by 1995 the amount of foreign exchange trading had grown to over fifteen times the amount required to service the country's import and export trading. It is this speculative surge that has knit together national markets for financial capital to form one global capital market.

In 1989, the Bank of International Settlements included foreign exchange trading in its formal data gathering for all central banks. Figure 5.1 shows that foreign exchange trading *on a daily basis* increased from US$590 billion in 1989 to US$3.2 trillion in 2007. In 1995 it already amounted to more than all the reserves of all the central banks of all the industrialized nations put together.

The significance is one of scale. In the past, financial activity was regulated by national institutions. Each country, through its central bank, shaped the money supply and regulated interest rates according to the priorities set by each respective government. Central banks advised national governments on the policies and regulations needed to support and protect the economic system. These agencies consulted with each other to share information, and they cooperated in the interest of economic stability. But a market on a global scale outstrips the power of any single national government to regulate its activities. This was demonstrated forcefully in 1992 when a hedge fund run by George Soros made a US$10-billion bet against the value of the British pound, forcing the Chancellor of the Exchequer to devalue that currency. In 1993 I asked then governor of the Bank of Canada, John Crow, how long his bank would be able to hold out if there was a run on the Canadian dollar. He replied that, if he had the support of all the other central banks of the largest economies, he could last only three weeks.

In July 1997 there was a speculative attack on the currencies of Thailand, Indonesia, the Philippines, Malaysia and South Korea. Thailand was forced to float its currency, which previously had been pegged to the U.S. dollar. Within a year, the Thai baht was worth 40 percent less than it had been. The Indonesian rupiah was devalued by over 80 percent in the same period. Not

Figure 5.1 Daily Global Value of Foreign Exchange Transactions

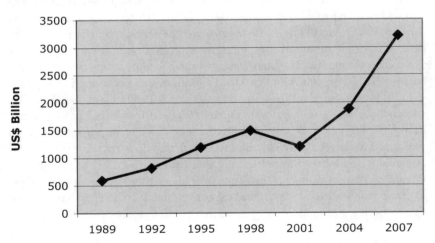

Source: The numerical values for this chart are as follows: 1989 – US$590b; 1992 – US$820b; 1995 – US$1190b; 1998 – US$1490b; 2001 – US$1200b; 2004 – US$1880b; 2007 – US$3210b. All figures taken from data supplied by the Bank of International Settlements 1995 & 2007.

surprisingly, Malaysian Prime Minister Mahathir Mohammed accused the West, particularly George Soros, of orchestrating this attack, though this has never been proven.

Hedge funds were now so large that they could dictate policy to governments. However, a second problem also emerged, and it still remains unsolved. Hedge funds are not regulated as tightly as commercial banks, or even mutual funds, and have become so large that their failure creates potentially fatal risks for other institutions. For example, in 1993 John Meriwether created a hedge fund called Long Term Capital Management (LTCM). Meriwether was the former head of bond trading at the Wall Street investment bank Salomon Brothers. He recruited to his board two Nobel Prize-winning economists with expertise in options trading, namely Robert Merton and Myron Scholes. LTCM made its money exploiting small pricing differences in international bonds. It also invested heavily in interest-rate derivatives. LTCM was highly successful in some years, earning a 40 percent annual return in 1995 and 1996. In order to make these kinds of returns it relied on leverage (borrowed money). Whereas commercial banks are required by international agreement to loan out no more than twenty times their reserve capital, investment banks typically loan out up to thirty times what they keep in reserve. LTCM was discovered to have borrowed and invested as much as a hundred times its capital (Tett 2009: 160). In 1998 it failed to anticipate a crisis in Russia when that country defaulted on some of its debt. The Clinton administration had to organize a bailout over the weekend to prevent all the major New York investment banks from going bankrupt as well because they were so heavily invested in LTCM (Cassidy 1999).[10] I say the problem has still not been solved because similar patterns were evident in the financial crisis of 2008.

The Crash of 2008

The New York Stock Exchange charted a loss of US$1.2 trillion on Monday, September 28, 2008 (Twin 2008). This was the largest dollar value loss in history, even though the 7 percent decline didn't make the top-ten list in terms of percentage losses. For this reason, people think of the recent economic collapse as a 2008 event. If we wanted to be more precise we could refer to the economic events of 2007–2009 as a single phenomenon. In the summer of 2007, commercial banks, investment banks and hedge funds around the world were hit by a collapse of mortgage-backed securities originating in the U.S. Rising defaults on these securities and the derivative products based on them caused financial institutions to begin hoarding cash and refusing to lend money to one another. Between July 2007 and March 2008, "Wall Street investment banks and brokerages hemorrhaged US$175 billion of capital" (Blackburn 2008: 63).

One of the first casualties was in the U.K. On September 13, 2007, the

British bank Northern Rock (the Rock) announced that it was appealing to the Bank of England for emergency support. It had formed in 1965 after the merger of two building societies dating back to the nineteenth century, and it had been owned by its members. It de-mutualized in the 1990s and then was traded on the London Stock Exchange. Based in Newcastle, it wasn't associated with Wall Street, subprime mortgages or even the financial district of the City of London. It specialized in mortgage loans to U.K. families and held the savings of British consumers. What it had in common with failing U.S. banks, though, was that earlier in the decade it had starting turning its mortgages into securities and selling them as if they were bonds. In addition, it used new accounting procedures that meant it was not required to reserve any of its own capital in case its borrowers defaulted. This allowed it to lend three times as much money as before, and sure enough, by 2007, it had increased its share of the U.K. mortgage market by three times, to over 18 percent (Tett 2009: 198). When the credit markets started to seize up, the Rock started to run out of money for the financing of its own operations, and no one was willing to buy new shares in the bank. In other words, it couldn't refinance its capital base, and it experienced a liquidity crisis. After the announcement was made, depositors started clamouring to withdraw their savings. This started a classic bank run, and four days later the government announced it would guarantee all bank deposits and provide enough loans to keep the bank operating.

The initial loan was £2 billion but it quickly escalated to £26 billion, an amount so large that the Office of National Statistics announced that it would now be treating Northern Rock as a public corporation and adding the loan to the national debt. On February 17, 2008, the Chancellor of the Exchequer made this appearance a reality by announcing that Northern Rock would be nationalized.

Global banks were estimated to have US$3.4 trillion held in reserve, so the American Federal Reserve (the Fed) was confident in early 2007 that a loss of US$100 billion would not endanger the banking system (Tett 2009: 208). Further investigation, however, showed that large loans were held in such a way that they did not fully appear in the books. This allowed the banks to be in technical compliance with regulations (the international Basel Accords) but still exposed them to enormous risk. These were derivatives of mortgage-backed securities held in special purpose vehicles and structured investment vehicles, and backed by various insurance companies. In American circles these became known as "troubled assets," which is why the government bailout program was known as the Troubled Asset Relief Program. In late 2007 the Federal Reserve began to pressure banks to increase their reserve capital. The obvious way to do that is by seeking new investors.

Earlier in the decade, China, Singapore, Korea and the oil producing

"The term subprime has become all too familiar as a result of the current credit crisis, which is attributed in part to the proliferation of subprime loans—loans made on unfavourable terms to borrowers unable to qualify for conventional loans. While researching the term, OED editors were surprised to discover an earlier financial sense, with quite the opposite meaning. The familiar current sense is attested only from 1993, but as early as 1976, sub-prime was being used to describe an especially desirable type of loan, one which charged less than the prime rate of interest and was offered only to the most reliable commercial borrowers. That meaning is now rare, and in the new sense which has replaced it, it is not the interest rate of the loan which is "less than prime," but the rating of the borrowers themselves." — Oxford English Dictionary 2008

countries of the Middle East had created what became known as "sovereign wealth funds." These were investment funds managing huge pools of government money. They were estimated to hold over US$3 trillion in 2007, normally in U.S. Treasury bonds and other safe assets.

> In late November the Abu Dhabi Investment Fund, the world's biggest sovereign wealth fund, announced plans to inject $7.5 billion into [Citibank]. Soon after, UBS raised $11 billion from the GIC fund of Singapore and Middle Eastern investors.[11] Then Merrill Lynch raised $5 billion from a Chinese government fund, while Morgan Stanley garnered a similar amount from Singapore. (Tett 2009: 210)

The commercial and investment banks increased their capital reserves but they also announced write-downs of their mortgage-backed assets. These announcements caused fear among investors, who then put their holdings of these same assets up for sale, causing the prices to drop even further. It was a vicious cycle. One of the first institutions to hit the wall was the investment brokerage Bear Stearns. Bear Stearns had had two hedge funds collapse in June 2007 and was unable to secure new financing from the Chinese investors it approached. CEO Jimmy Cayne resigned at the beginning of 2008 after the company reported a US$854-million loss. Investors began withdrawing their assets from the company and the cost of buying insurance against a default by Bear Stearns increased sixfold. On March 5, Bear Stearns's cash holdings exceeded US$20 billion. Five days later they had dropped to US$18 billion, and one day after that they plummeted to US$10 billion (Tett 2009: 218).

One of the differences between a commercial bank and a brokerage or an investment bank is the level of regulation. The Federal Reserve Board is a regulator of commercial banks, not stock brokerages. However, when Timothy Geithner, then head of the New York Federal Reserve Bank, heard

> "Quite apart from whether they were 'too big to fail,' they were too interconnected to ignore." — Tett 2009: 225

of Bear Stearns's troubles on Wednesday, March 12, 2008, he knew the brokerage was so tightly interconnected with the rest of the banking system that a failure would have widespread negative repercussions. In 2007 the New York Federal Reserve Bank calculated that the part of the banking system *outside its control* (sometimes called the "shadow banking system") was 40 percent larger than the component of the banking system for which it was responsible.

Two days later JP Morgan Chase, a commercial bank over which the Federal Reserve did have authority, announced that it was extending a US$30-billion loan to Bear Stearns using money made available by the Fed. On the Sunday night of that week, JP Morgan Chase agreed to buy Bear Stearns at a price of $2/share when it had traded on Friday at about $18 a share.[12] This valued the company at less than the value of its head office on Madison Avenue.

As 2008 progressed, so grew the estimated losses from mortgage-backed securities. This problem was no longer measured in the $100–$150 billion range. The International Monetary Fund now estimated losses of US$1 trillion (Blackburn 2008: 70). On September 7, 2008, the Federal Reserve put the Federal Home Loan Mortgage Corporation (FHLMC: Freddie Mac) and the Federal National Mortgage Association (FNMA: Fannie Mae) under conservatorship. These were two independent but government-sponsored enterprises specializing in home mortgages, and basically the government took them over. After reporting massive losses their share values fell by 50 percent. The Treasury invested US$100 billion in each enterprise in return for stock and warrants worth 80 percent of the companies' value.

The next week it was Lehman Brothers that was in crisis. In June the investment bank had announced a second quarter loss of US$2.8 billion. It was able to raise additional capital over the summer, and other funds continued to buy Lehman debt, assuming that, in the event of disaster, Lehman Brothers would be rescued like Bear Stearns had been. It would be considered too big and too interconnected to fail. By September, though, other trading partners were demanding additional collateral to cover loans. The New York Federal Reserve president Tim Geithner tried to do for Lehman what he had done for Bear Stearns, only this time with the British bank Barclays in the JP Morgan Chase role. When the British government refused to cover potential Barclays losses (as Geithner had done for JP Morgan Chase), Barclays backed out. On Sunday, September 14, Lehman announced it was bankrupt. On the same day, Merrill Lynch announced it was being bought by Bank of America.

The dominoes were starting to fall. When Geithner went to the bankers to try to save Lehman Brothers, their response was "When are we going to talk about AIG?" American Insurance Group was the largest insurer of derivative products. In February of 2008 it announced that its auditors had discovered a "material weakness" in its accounts. This meant that AIG had not set aside sufficient reserves to meet its obligations in the event of a large number of claims against its insurance. It wouldn't be able to pay. In the summer of 2008 it became clear that AIG was holding US$560 billion of so-called "super-senior risk." These were derivatives that were supposed to be of the most secure kind, almost never defaulting. In mid September the largest ratings agencies warned that they might have to remove AIG's AAA credit rating because of the increased risk. This would create a new credit squeeze because even more collateral would now be required to back up the loans AIG used to operate. Money market funds, supposedly the safest of investments, were starting to lose large amounts of money—an unprecedented event. Many of these funds owned securities insured by AIG. Financial institutions in the U.S., Europe and across Asia owned corporate debt and mortgage securities insured through credit default swaps[13] sold by AIG (Tett 2009: 237).

As an insurance company AIG was mostly profitable, but it had one division most insurance companies don't have: a financial services division. This had lost US$18 billion in the first nine months of 2008. When the credit rating agencies demanded an extra US$14.5 billion in collateral, the company couldn't raise it in the markets. Its share price had fallen 94 percent over the year (Karnitshnig et al. 2008). Two days after Lehman was allowed to go bankrupt, the U.S. government reversed course and took control of AIG. They lent the company US$85 billion in return for a 79.9 percent equity stake. The company was indeed too big and too interconnected to fail. The move also underscored the reality that an insurance company had now become a keystone of the banking industry, because it had one division that effectively operated as an investment bank.

My hometown of Toronto provides another example of how interconnected is the world of international finance. In 2007 potential buyers lined up around the block for a chance to buy a condominium in a new eighty-story tower planned for the corner of Yonge Street and Bloor Street. This corner is one of the most high-profile intersections in Canada, and the tower would have been Toronto's tallest residential building. The developer was Bazis International, a firm based in Kazakhstan. Funding for the Cdn$450-million project had been arranged through Lehman Brothers of New York. Without doubt, Lehman planned to turn the loan into a security and resell it on global financial markets. When Lehman Brothers declared bankruptcy the deal fell apart. Because credit markets froze up simultaneously, Bazis was unable to refinance the loan and in August of 2009 it arranged to sell the site to a Toronto-based developer, Great Gulf Homes. As of the time of writing it is thought that a smaller tower will be built on the site sometime in the future (Fenlon 2009).

Banks, insurance companies and developers are not the only institutions to go bankrupt in the current crisis. Countries can also effectively go bankrupt. Consider Iceland. Iceland is a country with less than 400,000 inhabitants. Its largest industries have been fishing and aluminum smelting. Its banking industry grew up around the fishing industry and gradually expanded to service fishing-related industries in the North Atlantic. Under the influence of disciples of Milton Friedman, especially Davíð Oddsson, the prime minister from 1991 to 2004, the banking sector was deregulated. It subsequently expanded rapidly, especially through subsidiaries in other countries. Here is how Paul Thomsen of the International Monetary Fund explained it:

> Iceland allowed a very oversized banking system to develop—a banking system that significantly outstripped the authorities' ability to act as a lender of last resort when the system ran into trouble. Only a few years ago, Iceland had a banking system that was the normal size. But after the privatization of the banking sector was completed in 2003, the banks increased their assets from being worth slightly more than 100 percent of GDP to being worth close to 1,000 percent of GDP. When confidence problems intensified this fall, Iceland was one of the first victims because the market realized that the banking system was far too big relative to the size of the economy. As investors started to pull out, it quickly spilled over into trouble for the Icelandic króna. Within a week the three banks collapsed, the króna's value dropped by more than 70 percent, and the stock market lost more than 80 percent of its value. For a small economy that is totally dependent on imports, this was a crisis of huge proportions. (Andersen 2008)

One of the countries where Iceland's banks expanded was Great Britain. When the Icelandic government seized control of the three largest Icelandic banks in early October 2008, funds owned by Iceland's banks and held in British banks were frozen. As an example, U.K.'s IceSave bank, owned by Iceland's Landsbanki, had 300,000 U.K. customers. Icelandic banks held £1 billion, deposited by public bodies like county councils, charities and pension funds. The British government then froze the assets held by Landsbanki until the Icelandic government agreed to guarantee the deposits. This is an example of how the banking industry can outgrow its regulatory framework and cause great dangers to society. In this case the only solution was a US$2.1-billion loan announced by the IMF on October 24, 2008.

> Because of the banking crisis, Iceland has gone overnight from being
> one of the lowest indebted countries in Europe, to being among the
> highest indebted advanced countries in Europe: Taking care of the
> problems in the banking sector will probably cost the public sector
> about 80 percent of GDP. (Andersen 2008)

Conclusion

In this process of financial globalization, national financial markets have been linked to form a single global market for credit, debt and currency. This global market has become either deregulated by policy or insufficiently regulated through lack of attention. As a consequence, the corporations that dominate this market are now larger than the national governments that used to regulate them, and we have not yet invented the new global institutions that will be required to oversee this new market. For example, Fortis Bank was the largest retail bank in Belgium. It took three countries (Belgium, Luxembourg and the Netherlands) to rescue it when it foundered in late September 2008. Iceland has had to be rescued by the International Monetary Fund after its largest banks failed. The largest Icelandic bank had assets six times larger than the GDP of the whole country. Could Switzerland rescue UBS, which has assets 484 percent larger than that country's GDP? Credit Suisse is 290 percent larger than its home country's GDP, as is ING in relation to the Netherlands. Three of the five largest banks in the world are headquartered in the U.K. (RBS, HSBC and Barclays). Britain has already rescued the Royal Bank of Scotland. Can it afford to rescue the other two?

The corporate agents of the national financial sectors of our economies have become disembedded from the regulatory frameworks of the nation-state (they were deregulated) and disembedded from the earlier moral consensus. They now exist in a new space called the globalized economy. They are so unstable and therefore so threatening to human society that even as prominent a champion of free market capitalism as George W. Bush was prepared to nationalize his banking sector to prevent further destruction.

When economic organizations are becoming disembedded from the restraints of the old society, there emerge champions of deregulation—"let the market decide," they cry. They are advocating a new moral justification. In the late eighteenth century it was Adam Smith who argued that if everyone was simply left to pursue their own self-interest, those actions would be guided, as if by "an invisible hand," to achieve the common good of wealth creation.

The social upheavals associated with the implementation of policies based on the rule of the invisible hand included market-induced famines, periodic shocks of industrial unemployment, dramatic increases in the gap between rich and poor, homelessness and waves of human migration as landless farmers sought to escape their poverty traps. William Blake described this in verse, and Charles Dickens described it in prose.

In the late twentieth century, at the time of the globalization revolution, it was Milton Friedman who argued that markets freed from regulation were a precondition for human freedom in a modern society. We are currently living through the social upheavals associated with the implementation of these policies of market deregulation. As the middle gets hollowed out and the majority of earners reap a decreasing share of the nation's income, more and more people get squeezed to the margins of society and become excluded from meaningful social participation. Unsurprisingly, conservative think tanks like Canada's Fraser Institute and the U.S.'s Heritage Foundation were celebrating Iceland as one of the freest countries in the world. We have seen the consequences of that kind of freedom.

The solution to the chaos caused by disembedded markets is obviously the re-embedding of those markets in new systems of political regulation with a new moral justification. That's one of the preconditions for an economy to become a moral economy. Where might those new systems of political regulation come from? In November 2008, leaders of the twenty largest national economies met in Washington for a summit to plan a response to the global financial crisis. What was symbolically significant about this meeting was that it is no longer sufficient for the leaders of the seven (now eight) largest national economies (the G7—now G8) to meet, consider and decide for the world, as they have done so often in the past. It is neither politically nor economically feasible to make decisions about world trade without China, India and Brazil being at the table—and they will not be silent. Some commentators called this meeting the new Bretton Woods, recalling the meeting in New Hampshire in 1944. Expectations were too grand for this 2008 meeting, but the hope was and is well placed. It may be that this meeting will set the wheels in motion and we may, in time, look back on it as the start of a new Great Transformation (see Eatwell & Taylor 2000).

One additional issue to consider regarding the parallel I have drawn between the Industrial Revolution and the Globalization Revolution is whether this also marks the birth of a new class structure. Some commentators argue that a new global capitalist class has now been formed (Sklair 2001; Carroll 2007). This class is comprised of those who own or control transnational corporations along with the merchants, politicians, bureaucrats and other professionals who support them. This corresponds to the new capitalist class formed in the Industrial Revolution that displaced the rulers of the old agriculturally based feudal society. Following the analyses of Karl Polanyi and E.P. Thompson, our question then becomes: what new class will become conscious as part of the double movement? If social relations have now become globalized, do not the structures of the nation state become analogous to the common-law structures of the feudal order? Can we not see populations calling on the old moral consensus that was built on the basis of the nation-state at the same time as new global structures of regulation are being fashioned? What popular alliances can be created globally that will help to resist the restructuring, in the interests of capital, that pushes large parts of the population to the margins of society, and will the resistance be only negative?

If the people are to intervene, by what values will this intervention be guided? Let me suggest four such values:

Matthew's Gospel (7:26) reminds us to build our houses on a solid foundation, not on sand. That means our financial systems, like our ecological systems, have to be *sustainable*.

In order for the system to be sustainable, we have to be clear about what is *sufficient* for our common life. So far we have organized our affairs to achieve the maximum growth possible. What would "enough" look like?

Most people want some basic standards of fairness applied to income and employment, hence the desire to limit CEO pay for companies receiving public financial aid. This is the principle of *equity*.

Finally, ordinary people are wondering why government money goes to rescuing private investors when ordinary homeowners are underwater. They are looking for some collective support. They are looking for *solidarity*.

Notes

1. Home ownership rates in the U.S. increased from 65 percent in 1981 to 69 percent in 2006. "Census Bureau Reports on Residential Vacancies and Homeownership," U.S. Census Bureau, October 26, 2007.

2. In 2004 the *Washington Post* reported that the number of factory workers in the U.S. had declined by 5 million in the last twenty-five years for this reason. See "As Income Gap Widens, Uncertainty Spreads," *Washington Post*, September 19, 2004.

3. There is a virtual academic industry disputing the dating of the Industrial Revolution, and even whether it should be described as revolutionary or something more gradual. I am dating it from 1775, the year James Watt obtained a patent for the design of his improved steam engine.

4. For the sake of argument I have greatly simplified the description of the Industrial Revolution here. I have excluded the impact of scientific approaches to agriculture, crop rotation and the like, and also glossed over its different stages. For a comprehensive review see Stearns 1998.

5. In 1809 John Molson was successfully running a steamer between Montreal and Quebec City, the first steamer on the St. Lawrence.

6. Some people consider the key technology to be the transistor, invented in 1947, which is used in computer chips.

7. Jack Kilby was awarded the Nobel Prize in 2000 for his role in this invention. Another person credited with the invention was Robert Noyce of Fairfield

Semiconductor. He invented his version six months later but made his with silicon, which proved to be a big improvement on Kilby's use of germanium.

8. There are other explanations for the oil shock of 1973. The most common one is that it was an Arab reaction to American support for Israel after the Arab-Israeli War that same year.

9. The Chicago Mercantile Exchange started in the nineteenth century as the Chicago Butter and Egg Board. It merged with the Chicago Board of Trade in 2007 and became known as the CME Group. In 2008 it merged with the New York Mercantile Exchange.

10. LTCM operated thereafter under supervision and was closed down in 2000.

11. UBS AG is a Swiss bank formed in 1998 by a merger of Union Bank of Switzerland, based in Zurich, with the Swiss Bank Corporation, based in Basel. GIC is a global investment management company established in 1981 to manage Singapore's foreign currency reserves.

12. At the insistence of the New York Federal Reserve Bank, JP Morgan Chase was forced to increase its price for Bear Stearns from $2 to $10/share.

13. A credit default swap is a kind of insurance against a debt default. For example, a bank might invest in a large corporate bond issue. It would then sign a contract with a third party (like AIG) against the possibility that the corporation issuing the bond would fail to pay when the bond was due. AIG would have to pay the full amount of the contract in that case, but would receive regular premiums for this guarantee in the meantime.

6. Ethics, Globalization and the Common Good

In the previous chapter I focused on the economic dimension of globalization. However, the ethical dimension of globalization has been revealed more clearly in the political realm. Over the last thirty to forty years a new international political regime has emerged and asked us to bless economic globalization. That is, the new regime has asked that we accept that economic globalization is the answer to our problems and not a problem for which we need an answer. We are asked to embrace globalization and to have a clean conscience in doing so.

This new international political regime has had several names. It is most commonly called neoliberalism, though for some years it was called neoconservatism because it was being advanced by political parties describing themselves as conservative. The "liberal" component of neoliberalism does not refer to contemporary political parties that describe themselves as liberal, but rather to the nineteenth-century liberal movement that advocated laissez-faire policies. Included within this discourse is the Washington Consensus. The term "Washington Consensus" was coined in 1990 by John Williamson "to refer to the lowest common denominator of policy advice being addressed by the Washington-based institutions to Latin American countries as of 1989," though it is often used interchangeably with the term "neo-liberal policies" (Williamson 2000).

Some people associate this regime with the rise to power of U.S. President Ronald Reagan (1981–89), while others associate it with the rise to power of U.K. Prime Minister Margaret Thatcher (1979–90). Still others associate it with the military coup that overthrew Chilean President Salvador Allende, killing him, on Sept. 11, 1973. The military government which followed, led by General Augusto Pinochet, initiated sweeping economic changes based on advice given by followers of University of Chicago economist Milton Friedman (Klein 2007: 87). What these three political figures have in common is they used their political power to force a deregulation of economic sectors. They claimed that market forces were being hampered by government regulation and so moved to liberate those forces and encourage global economic integration. As Ronald Reagan said in his first inaugural address on January 20, 1981: "In this present crisis, government is not the solution to our problem; government is the problem."

This is what I mean when I say that for the last thirty or forty years we have been asked to bless this process of globalization. We have been told that we all need to become more competitive because we need to conform our behaviour to the demands of the "free market." We are asked to accept those free markets as if they were somehow external to our social life, even though we have actually deregulated them in order to encourage competition.

Competition is not a bad thing necessarily, as long as it goes hand-in-hand with other moral values. As I have tried to illustrate with various stories, competition needs to be accompanied by the virtues of trust, honesty and a view to the general welfare of others—in other words, justice. When it stands alone it can become demonic.

Ethics as a word can be understood to mean theories of morality. However, in common discourse the words ethics and morality are often used interchangeably. That is how I am using the word here. In this sense all ethics are guides for action. When competition is the only value that guides your behaviour, it turns into domination because the activity of competition is not a one-off event. It is a recurring, indeed never-ending process. Competition in the context of scarcity produces permanent winners and losers. If I am competing with you then that means I want to win and I want you to lose. Since the competition is never-ending, that means I want to win today, to-morrow, next week and next year. If competition is the only ethic guiding my behaviour, then my domination of you is the state I am trying to achieve. As many commentators have noted, competition among firms within a capitalist economy tends toward the domination of any given market by one or a very small number of firms. When one firm dominates we call this monopoly. When a few firms dominate, we call it oligopoly.

Actions are guided by rules of behaviour (ethics), but they are sustained by attitudes. This activity of domination can only be sustained if you adopt an attitude of indifference toward your neighbour. If you have compassion toward your neighbours, you will want to stand in solidarity with them when they are troubled. You will want to cooperate with them to find a solution to their suffering. I have diagrammed this relationship in Table 6.1.

Competition is commonly described as a characteristic of corporations. Companies compete with each other within a given economic sector. Even

Table 6.1: The Ethics of Globalization

though some say the term is improperly applied to countries (Heath 2009: 99), others argue that countries do compete with each other in the world market, and their success in doing so is one of the keys to prosperity (Porter 1990). The World Economic Forum has been publishing a Global Competitiveness Report since 1979. In the most recent report, Canada has moved up in the rankings to #9, from #10 in 2008 and #11 in 2007 (Schwab 2009). The United States ceded first place this year to Switzerland. The increasing use of competitiveness rhetoric encourages the adoption of competition as an overarching ethic. Even though economists and philosophers commonly defend themselves by saying they are only constructing models of behaviour and they don't expect them to fully correspond to actual behaviour, still some studies have shown that emphasizing competition as a guiding principle actually creates competitive behaviour. For example, in a 1993 study researchers found that not only were economists less cooperative than non-economists, but that differences in cooperativeness were caused in part by their training in economics (Frank, Gilovitch & Regan 1993).

When we describe the ethics of globalization as an ethics of competition, the comparison with athletic events comes immediately to mind. The overwhelming emphasis on competition in high-profile sporting events has led many athletes to rely on drugs to give them a competitive advantage. The Canadian runner Ben Johnson had his 1988 Olympic 100-metre gold medal rescinded because of steroid use. U.S. track star Marion Jones won three gold and two bronze medals at the 2000 Olympic Games in Sydney. She was subsequently barred from the Beijing games and stripped of her medals after she admitted to using steroids before the Sydney Games. She was also convicted of perjury and imprisoned in Texas.

The Tour de France is the most famous cycling race in the world. It currently operates under a dark cloud because drug cheating is so widespread. Tour champion Floyd Landis has been discredited in spite of his denials. Several corporate sponsors have refused to back their teams, and now whole teams have quit the race after their riders were caught blood doping. The American satirical magazine *The Onion* has started selling versions of the yellow bracelets made popular by cycling champions. Their bracelets read "Cheat to Win."

Can competitive sports ever be ethical? Let me tell two stories that suggest the answer is yes. The Velux 5 Oceans yacht race covers 30,140 nautical miles and is held once every four years, just like the Olympics. In 2006, in the middle of the Southern Ocean, British racer Alex Thomson was in third place when his boat overturned, causing irreparable damage to his keel. His nearest competitor was Mike Golding, eighty miles ahead of him in second place. Mike Golding turned his boat around and sailed back to perform a very complicated rescue.

Mike Golding's actions were not unprecedented. This kind of accident is common enough in sailing that assistance is obligatory. Failure to assist is grounds for disqualification. Mutual assistance is part of what it means to be excellent in sailing (Sailing Networks Website 2006).

In April 2008, the Western Oregon Wolves were playing the second game of their softball doubleheader against the Central Washington Wildcats. The winner would proceed to the division championships. In the second inning, with two runners on base, Wolves outfielder Sara Tucholsky hit the first home run of her college career. In her excitement she neglected to touch first base. As she turned around to retrace her steps, her knee buckled and she lay on the ground writhing in pain.

Softball rules prevent a player's teammates from helping her to round the bases. Acting on instinct, Wildcat first-basewoman Mallory Holtman looked at shortstop Liz Wallace, and together they carried Tucholsky around the bases, allowing her to touch her one good leg to each one. The Western Oregon Wolves ended up winning the game 4–2 and went on to the NCAA tournament (Vecsey 2008).

Cooperation has a long history as the defining feature of a different approach to economics. In the U.K., a fire insurance cooperative was organized in the early 1700s. A cheesemakers cooperative was organized in France around 1750. With the work of English social reformer Robert Owen and the creation of the Rochdale Society in the U.K. in the early nineteenth century, and the work of French theorist Charles Gide in the late nineteenth century, cooperative societies started to take off and have now been formed throughout the world. Over 91 million Americans belonged to credit unions in 2005 (NCBA nd), but Canada has the highest per-capita credit union membership in the world with 33 percent of Canadians belonging to at least one credit union (CCA nd).

India has the largest cooperative movement, with over 166 million members in 1991 (Williams 2007: 12). So, you may not be surprised to know that in 1976 Professor Muhammad Yunus launched a cooperatively based action research program in Bangladesh aimed at reducing poverty by extending credit to the poorest of the poor (Grameen, the name of the bank, means "rural" or "village" in the local Bangla language).

The Grameen system is compellingly simple. A group of five prospective borrowers is formed. Only two can receive the first loan, and the whole team ensures that the loan is repaid since only then are the others able to borrow money. No collateral is used other than the trust offered by the community. A track record is quickly established, and borrowers who successfully repay the first loan can then borrow larger amounts. The first loan made was for $27. Since 1983 the Grameen bank has lent $5.1 billion to 5.3 million people and adds more than 1 percent annually to the gross domestic product of Bangladesh.

Some realities are hidden by these figures. Dr. Yunus's action research project became a bank through government legislation and received support from both the central bank and the nationalized commercial banks. The Grameen bank is 90 percent owned by the poor whom it serves, with the government owning the remaining 10 percent. Most of the borrowers are women and the loan repayment rate is 95 percent. This is a marvelous achievement, and in 2006 Professor Yunus was honoured with a Nobel Prize for his work.

However, Professor Yunus is merely symbolic of the extraordinary efforts made by cooperative leaders around the world who don't get the same publicity but do the same kind of work.

Father Greg MacLeod is a Catholic Priest who grew up in Cape Breton, an economically depressed but socially vibrant part of Nova Scotia. In 1976 he created a community development corporation named New Dawn Enterprises. One of its first challenges was to deal with the shortage of dentists on the island of Cape Breton. New Dawn built and equipped a dental clinic and then persuaded a newly graduated dentist to occupy it. The young dentist was attracted because he didn't need to borrow money to establish himself. New Dawn then repeated this process until Cape Breton had established a good reputation as a place to practise dentistry. Over twenty-five years the number of dentists on the island increased from two to seventy.

New Dawn also responded when a local rope factory was being sold and relocated to the United States. The factory was built with government money and locals thought they should have a chance to revive it before it was taken away. The women of the community blockaded the factory site and prevented it from being removed, and New Dawn negotiated the purchase. The rope factory is now a thriving commercial venture. Today, there are ten different companies operating under New Dawn Enterprises, with assets of $20 million.

Both Professor Yunus and Father MacLeod have demonstrated that when communities get behind an idea they bring something to the table that has real value. This is called "social capital." It is as valuable as financial capital, but you won't find it under the mattress. You find it in your community relationships.

The cooperative movement has also generated political movements. For example, in Canada the Cooperative Commonwealth Federation (CCF) was started in 1932. In 1961 it made a formal alliance with the labour union movement and changed its name to the New Democratic Party (NDP). At one time or another this party has formed the government in five of Canada's ten provinces.

However, as the word "commonwealth" implies, any vision for an ethics of globalization based on the contrast between competition and cooperation also draws our attention to a larger shared ethical vision. One way or another it stands on some notion of a good that we hold in common—that is, a vision of the common good.

The Idea of a Common Good

Philosophers typically trace the language of the common good back to Aristotle. In his *Nicomachean Ethics*, Aristotle concerned himself with what it means to live a good life. He concluded that a human life can be considered good if it is organized around the pursuit of goals that were good or fitting. The habits of life that tended towards these goals were described as virtues and these goals were considered the end (telos) of an action in the same way that an acorn has within it the telos of an oak tree. His approach to ethics is described as a "teleological" approach. "One of Aristotle's most significant conclusions was that a good life is oriented to goods shared with others—the common good of the larger society of which one is a part" (Hollenbach 2002: 3).

In contemporary Western thought, the language of the common good has fallen into disfavour. Rather than a foundation or a call to unity, the language of the common good is now thought of as an invitation to conflict—sometimes armed conflict. In political terms, it is associated with the coercive imposition of the will of one group over another, all under the cover of the notion of a general will. In the words of liberal political theorist John Rawls, "a public and workable agreement on a single and general comprehensive conception [of the good] could be maintained only by the oppressive use of state power" (Rawls 1987: 4). Some people trace the rejection of the language of the common good to the religious wars that convulsed Europe during and after the Reformation. For others it is a result of the development of the same liberal theory that interprets the functioning of the marketplace as enabling the hand of God. Regardless of its origins, the dominant philosophy in the West now assumes that there is no single good but only a plethora of goods, and it is not up to the state to determine what is good. Instead, it is up to each individual to decide what is good or bad and govern their actions accordingly. Where the language of the common good remains, it is understood to mean simply the aggregation of individual goods chosen by all people. In other words, the common good has been reduced to the greatest good for the greatest number—John Stuart Mill's classic formulation of utilitarianism. In its extreme form, politics can no longer be concerned with anything like a common good since anyone advancing any particular cause is simply competing for a private interest. Debates about what goods we might have in common are then replaced by an affirmation of tolerance for these infinite differences.

Some contemporary democratic theorists propose a third way to transcend the choice between coercion and disengaged coexistence. Amy

Gutmann and Dennis Thompson, for example, recommend the principle of "deliberative democracy" as a way forward: "when citizens or their representatives disagree morally, they should continue to reason together to reach mutually acceptable decisions" (Gutmann & Thompson 1996: 62). This approach starts from the assumption of moral disagreement rather than common conviction about visions of the good life, and develops processes likely to achieve consensus.

However, there is another source to which we can turn to help us think about a moral vision humans might have in common. The great religions of the world have long maintained a vision of a common good. There are many ways it is expressed or alluded to but probably the most common is the "Golden Rule." Its ethical import is typically expressed as "Do unto others as you would have them do unto you" and finds its Christian reference in the Gospel of Matthew (7:12), although many religions have a version of it. For example, in one of the most popular Hindu Scriptures, the Mahabharata, we find the following injunction: "One should never do that to another which one regards as injurious to one's own self. This, in brief, is the rule of dharma" (Mahabharata Online. n.d). This particular rule is sometimes described as an ethic of reciprocity. A Roman Catholic religious order claims that thirteen religions share this ethic, but others say more than twenty do (see Scarboro Missions Website n.d.).

Another common Christian reference is the story of the Good Samaritan (Luke 10: 25–37). Because of this heritage, religious organizations continue to use the language of the common good. The Roman Catholic Church has been the most systematic in its development of the idea.[1] This tradition has recently been reviewed by the U.S. Jesuit theologian David Hollenbach, who was one of the staff members responsible for drafting the 1986 pastoral letter on economic justice put out by the U.S. Conference of Catholic Bishops. One of his reasons for writing *The Common Good and Christian Ethics* was his experience with the public response to the pastoral letter. He was surprised to learn "that a central concept being advanced by the bishops' letter—the common good—was nearly incomprehensible to most of the people the bishops sought to address." Ten years later he found himself teaching at a college in Kenya with students drawn from all over sub-Saharan Africa. Some of the students came from groups and nations at war with other groups and nations represented in the same classroom. This second experience convinced him that developing an understanding of the common good that is plausible in a diverse society was not only possible but also necessary (Hollenbach 2002: xiii).

In trying to overcome the lack of comprehension among U.S. audiences, Hollenbach finds it necessary to overcome the paradigm of tolerance as the only way of understanding how democracy can function. To introduce this paradigm he quotes Ronald Dworkin's conviction that equal treatment of

citizens demands that "political decisions must be, so far as possible, independent of any particular conception of the good life" (Dworkin 1985: 191). It
is not a shared understanding of the good that binds us together but rather
a willingness to tolerate a diversity of viewpoints.

From Hollenbach's point of view, the Catholic tradition of the common
good already incorporates the principle of diversity. The Christian theologian Thomas Aquinas was incorporating the non-Christian philosophy of
Aristotle. He also learned from the great Jewish philosopher Maimonides and
the great Islamic scholars Ibn Sina (Avicenna) and Ibn Rusd (Averroes). He
didn't rely on the existence of a common religion or a common culture but
rather on the power of a common human reason that is capable of grasping
the broad outlines of a common good (Hollenbach 2002: 13).

By the same token Hollenbach takes for granted that our understanding of the common good can develop over time. Aristotle excluded women,
slaves and resident aliens (*metics*) from the rights of citizenship whereas our
modern understanding of the equal dignity of all persons demands a politics of inclusion. Today, it is our increased interdependence that demands
a rethinking of classical notions of the common good. "We cannot simply
invoke Aristotle or Aquinas for solutions to our problems. Their world is
vastly different from ours and one hopes we have actually learned something
from the intervening centuries" (Hollenbach 2002: 60).

The reference to the equal dignity of persons is significant here. The
equal dignity of persons is a reflection of the theological affirmation (common to Judaism, Christianity and Islam) that all human beings are made
in the image of God.[2] This affirmation of the fundamental dignity of all
human beings is shared with more secular affirmations like the Universal
Declaration of Human Rights. The use of the word "person" rather than
"individual" is no accident, for in the tradition of Catholic social teaching a
person is more than a consumer or a producer—more even than a citizen.
A person is a social being, embedded in and constituted by relationships.
This means that each person is part of some greater whole. The good of
the whole cannot be calculated by finding an arithmetical sum of individual
goods. By the same token, persons are not merely parts of that whole like
cogs in a large machine. "The relation between the good of persons and the
common good is more complex than the mathematical operations of division
or summation can represent" (Hollenbach 2002: 69).

To say that a person is not merely a cog in a machine is to recognize that
the common will has the capacity to be demonic. That is, tyranny, oppression
and war are social "bads" that need to be defended against. An adequate
understanding of the common good requires a minimum threshold of freedom and mutual respect along with the social practices and institutions that
make these possible. Hollenbach identifies with the Canadian philosopher

Charles Taylor in describing this freedom as a "situated freedom." That is, it is not just a solitary, isolated freedomi but rather the freedom that comes from being self-determining and therefore engaged, initiating, responsive and dissenting (Taylor 1989: 519). Taylor also describes this as "freedom in community."

The contemporary Catholic understanding of the common good described by Hollenbach as "dialogic universalism" is:

> It is universalist, for it presumes that human beings are sufficiently alike in that they all share certain very general characteristics in common and that the same general outlines of well-being are shared in common as well. For example, the good of all human beings requires that basic bodily needs be met, that intelligence be developed and educated, that freedom of conscience be respected, and that participation in social and political life be a real possibility. At the same time the pursuit of the common good is dialogic. Cultural differences are so significant that a shared vision of the common good can only be attained in a historically incremental way through deep encounter and intellectual exchange across traditions. It is also dialogic because it sees engagement with others across the boundaries of traditions as itself part of the human good. (Hollenbach 2002: 152)

This approach assumes that when freedoms are exercised in dialogue with others a common life comes into existence even though this occurs in the midst of diversity. This common life becomes an expression of solidarity, even as it also serves as solidarity's prerequisite. In this sense the common good is a goal of ethical action, and solidarity is a virtue, a habit of ethical practice, that will help get us there. Indeed, Hollenbach points to the declaration of Pope John Paul II, calling for solidarity to be added to the list of cardinal virtues (prudence, justice, temperance and fortitude) and theological virtues (faith, hope and love), as "a firm and persevering determination to commit oneself to the common good" (Pope John Paul II, *Sollicitudo Rei Socialis*, No. 38, in O'Brien and Shannon 1992). "One of the most important meanings of the concept of the common good," writes Hollenbach, "is that it is the good that comes into existence in a community of solidarity among active, equal agents" (Hollenbach 2002: 189).

The picture Hollenbach paints of a modernized version of the common good is a vision affirming universal human rights, because those rights presume the existence of a moral community to which all humans belong. Indeed, those human rights are the minimum requirement for participation in community. Solidarity is the (virtuous) ethical action that supports these rights and works for the goal of social inclusion. "The choice today is not between freedom and community, but between a society based on recipro-

cal respect and solidarity and a society that leaves many people behind"
(Hollenbach 2002: 244).

The Critique of the Common Good

Iris Marion Young was a U.S. political philosopher (1949–2006) who worked
at the intersection of justice, democracy, feminism, critical theory and public
policy. In her book *Inclusion and Democracy*, Young offered a critique of the
assumption made by some democratic theorists that either the common good
or common interests should be the focus of good democratic discussion:

> They assume that politics must be either a competition among pri-
> vate and conflicting interests, or that political participants must put
> aside their particular interests and affiliations to form a deliberative
> public.... I argue that this is a false dichotomy, and that a third pos-
> sibility is more plausible. (Young 2000: 7)

Young acknowledged that citizens have shared problems that require solutions. Her concern was to articulate and defend the principles of a democratic
politics that would be the most just way to solve those collective problems.
Because she was using the methods of critical theory, she was sceptical of
attempts to derive those principles from philosophical premises about the
nature of the good life. Instead she wanted to reflect on our experience of
existing social relations and institutional processes and identify what we find
valuable in them.

This reflection led her to focus on the values of self-determination and
self-development and the social and institutional arrangements that support
these values. Following the development economist Amartya Sen (see Sen
1985 and Nussbaum 2000), she understood self-development to mean the
development of capabilities—the ability "for all persons to learn and use
satisfying and expansive skills in socially recognized settings, and enable
them to play and communicate with others or express their feelings and
perspectives on social life in contexts where others can listen" (Young 2000:
31). These capabilities can also be understood as freedoms, not freedoms
in the negative sense as freedom from coercion, but freedom in the positive
sense as freedom to actually choose one's own future.

Because Young wants to reflect on actually existing democracies, she
focuses on the processes of imperfect democracies with real structural injus-
tices like inequalities of status, knowledge, wealth, and social and economic
power. Like other theorists she is an advocate of deliberative democracy, but
she is also a critic. What she criticizes is the affirmation of a common good,
either as a prior condition for or as a goal of deliberation.[3] She finds both
positions problematic.

Regarding the common good as a prior condition, she understands pluralist societies to have such deep divisions of gender, class and culture that assumptions of shared understanding are likely to be mistaken. Can we really assume that men and women of northern European, South Asian or African Canadian ancestries, who work in daycares or as lawyers, really have shared ideas about, and commitments to, what constitutes a common good if we don't first examine critically the extent to which our life experiences are really shared? Young would say no. She also thinks that assumptions of shared understanding deny the need for transformation that real dialogue across difference will produce. If we don't expect this transformation, we will only see in the other a mirror image of ourselves (Young 2000: 42).

Turning to the idea of the common good as a goal, Young is suspicious of any process that requires "differences of identity, culture, interests, social position, or privilege as something to be bracketed"(Young 2000: 42). Under conditions of social inequality, this version of the common good can become a means of exclusion. Similarly, it can silence some points of view if it narrows the agenda in such a way that some grievances are considered illegitimate. Any social and political debate requires a judgement about which issues will have urgent priority and which others will have to wait for later. Consider how often serious political debates about equal access to clean drinking water for indigenous communities get sidetracked by more popular but less significant issues concerning, for example, the personal ethics of individual politicians. Finally, Young argues, if conflict and disagreement are not considered a normal state of affairs then "too strong a commitment to consensus as a common good can incline some or all to advocate removing difficult issues from discussion for the sake of agreement and preservation of the common good" (Young 2000: 44).

As the title of her book, *Inclusion and Democracy*, implies, Iris Marion Young tries to account for difference and conflict within democratic processes. She starts with formally democratic societies under conditions of structural inequality. She recognizes that large segments of the population have experienced grotesque injustice. For example, indigenous peoples in North America have been "removed, dispersed, killed; their languages, religious practices, and artistic expression suppressed. They demand of the societies that continue to dominate them recognition and support for their distinct cultures and the freedom to express and rejuvenate those cultures" (Young 2000: 106). However, their identity as a single group, in this case "Indians," is an identity imposed from the outside. What they share is an experience of colonial oppression, again externally imposed. Internally, there is a wide diversity of identities, sometimes corresponding to historical political formations and sometimes not. What is lacking and what is desired is self-determination and self-development. By the same token, women can be identified as a group but some women deny or reject this basis for identity. Even "many French people deny the existence of a French identity and claim that being French is nothing particularly important to their personal identities" (Young 2000: 88).

Here she rejects the notion that there is anything "essential" in such a group identity. She rejects what she describes as "substantivist logic" and instead argues that groups need to be understood as constructed by "relational logic." The substantivist logic is a logic applied from the outside by people who attribute to a group an identity based on certain substantive attributes. Women have these attributes, for example, Anglos these other ones. In contrast, she argues that "individuals construct their own identities on the basis of social group positioning" (Young 2000: 82). Social structures can produce common experiences of injustice and oppression, and people may form a group for the purpose of redress. In this sense a group has no collective identity apart from the individuals in it. It is not a random aggregate of persons but rather the individuals and their relationships. In this she argues against others like Jean Bethke Elshtain, who claim that a politics of difference destroys public commitment to the common good (Elshtain 1995: 74).

In arguing to include conflict within an understanding of deliberative democracy, Young opposes those who assume a functioning democracy must enable civil discourse. For Young the latter means those who are suffering injustice are required to pretend they are not aggrieved. Their angry behaviour, rooted in their experience of injustice, is part of their difference. The norm of civility in an unjust society is a norm of silence and exclusion.

> When confronted so starkly with an opposition between difference and civility, most must opt for civility. But a conception of deliberative politics which insists on putting aside or transcending partial and particularist differences forgets or denies the lesson that the politics of difference claims to teach…. Under circumstances of structural social and economic inequality, the relative power of some groups often allows them to dominate the definition of the common good in ways compatible with their experience, perspective, and priorities. (Young 2000: 108–109)

Young is also responding to theorists who invoke the norm of the common good either as a way of determining a common identity or articulating a common goal. She rejects the efforts to find a shared identity if it means employing a substantivist logic to settle on common cultural attributes. She also rejects the efforts to articulate a common goal if that means requiring people to treat their grievances as particularities to be overcome in the interest of the general welfare. It is not enough, for example, to say that the general welfare is advanced when mercury is removed from the industrial process used to create paper from wood pulp. The grievances of specific populations who suffer from mercury poisoning must also be addressed.[4]

Young makes a case for inclusiveness, and that means she argues against any notion of a single public with a single discourse of the common good. Instead she argues for "a heterogeneous public engaged in transforming institutions to make them more effective in solving shared problems justly" (Young 2000: 12).

Inclusion, Coercion and Freedom

The differences between Hollenbach and Young are obvious, but their similarities may be all the more surprising for that. Both reject coercion as the means for achieving a common good, and both reject the idea that the common good can be built on a simple aggregation of individual goods. Both are concerned with understanding what correct behaviour looks like in a pluralistic society.

It may be that what Hollenbach understands as the constituent parts of the common good, Young considers the constituent parts of justice. For example, Hollenbach begins his defence of the common good with an affirmation of the moral equality of persons. This is clearly a development of thought since Aristotle, but Hollenbach is quick to acknowledge that concepts do and should develop over time. For Young, the moral equality of persons would be one of the building blocks of social justice. Hollenbach's understanding of "person" as a social category including the individual and her relationships matches Young's understanding of groups constituted by individuals and their relationships. The group members "stand in determinate relation both to one another and to non-members" (Young 2000: 90).

Hollenbach describes the Catholic tradition of the common good as one of dialogic universalism. He refers to it as dialogic because it takes cultural diversity so seriously that it demands a deep encounter across difference. And it is universalist because it makes certain universal claims about what it means to be human and what constitutes human well-being. For instance, human well-being requires a certain minimum level of participation in the life of the community, and this can be understood in turn as an argument in favour of free speech and political democracy.

Some critics will not be convinced by Hollenbach's characterization of Catholic tradition. Young's preference for a critical theory approach that examines actually existing institutions will aim to contrast this Catholic theory of the common good with the actually existing Roman Catholic Church, and its history and continuing practice of discrimination against women. In the same way, critics will distinguish the theoretical commitment to a deep encounter across cultures with the actual historical preference for European cultural forms in the church's institutional life.[5] On the other hand, Young's arguments for justice are also based on some prior conception of what it means to be human and what it means to develop one's capacity to flourish. Young bases her understanding of human flourishing on the work of Amartya Sen. Hollenbach relies on Charles Taylor to support his understanding of self-determination. Both develop notions of self-development based on conceptions of positive freedom. So, they may not be as far apart as one might think. Young even endorses the principle of subsidiarity to guide the relationship between local and global governance regimes. This is to say that organizational or administrative matters ought to be handled by the smallest or least centralized authority that is competent to do so. It is a long-standing and well-developed principle in Catholic social thought and has become a tenet of the European Union (Young 2000: 267).

David Hollenbach is not alone in defending the common good in this way. The U.S. Presbyterian ethicist Douglas Hicks argues for it in a very similar way, resting the concept on a primary affirmation of the moral equality of persons and elaborating the normatively significant needs of persons to realize their full and equal personhood. He relies on liberationist philosophers and theologians like Ignacio Ellacuria S.J. (1930–1989)[6] for support when he writes that "liberationists do not object to employing language of the common good" (Hicks 2000: 172). Their use of this language is conditional on a preferential option for the poor. Like Hollenbach, he argues that claims for particular goods assume the existence of a common good. But he also uses that formula to reject the attempts of the rich to claim for themselves goods (like housing and health care) that should properly belong to all. His support for the common good leads to "a society of egalitarian solidarity in which all people could have a genuine sense of stake" (Hicks 2000: 173).

In Hollenbach's defence of the common good he borrows from Charles Taylor the notion of "situated freedoms," which helps to explain the difference between negative and positive freedom and the significance of self-determination (see Taylor 1989). Freedoms that are only abstract are not real freedoms. They must have a concrete reality, they must be situated, to have effect. Iris Marion Young, in her defence of difference, borrows from Donna Haraway and other feminist theorists the notion of "situated knowledges," which helps to explain the need for the explicit voicing of different positions and experiences in order to achieve objectivity (see Haraway 1991). Hicks uses the term "situated selfhood" and makes the same link as does Young with the work of Amartya Sen. If there are normatively significant needs that must be satisfied in order to realize the freedom to be self-determining, what are they? "Sen emphasizes that the basic capability of a person is reflected in the set of basic functionings and freedoms that are available to her or him" (Hicks 2000: 192). Hicks then draws our attention to the human development reports prepared by the United Nations that have taken up Sen's language about human capabilities. For Hicks and Ellacuria, "the common good is basically a union of structural conditions that a society as a whole must provide for its citizens" (Hicks 2000: 173). These structural conditions must overcome oppression and allow for basic human flourishing.

The ethics of globalization pose a stark contrast between an ethic of competition and an ethic of cooperation. This is not an attempt to argue that competition is morally bad. Rather, it is an effort to point out that when competition is isolated from other moral values it can create conditions that lead to a denial of compassion, a rejection of solidarity and an abandonment of the common good.

The work of Iris Marion Young reminds us that we have reason to be suspicious of common good metaphors, especially where they encourage us to bracket differences of identity, culture, interests, social position or privilege. We do not yet live in a world free of structural inequality. So even as we struggle to resolve common problems we need to work hard to voice our differences and create the conditions of self-development for all.[7]

There are still some political theorists who use common good language to describe both a moral foundation and a moral goal. One context in which this language has never fallen out of use is in religious discourse, and we have already examined some Christian theologians for examples. It is important to remember that Christian theology also develops over time and in response to changing social, economic and political conditions. Contemporary understandings in Christian theology of the common good also take into account the politics of difference, more in the economic than the cultural realm, with special reference to the preferential option for the poor.

One of the ways in which Christian thinkers and activists want to use the idea of the common good is as a foundation for solidarity. As we have seen above, Pope John Paul II wanted to include solidarity in the conventional list of cardinal and theological virtues. I have already identified solidarity as the realization of a cooperative ethic and the opposite of an activity of domination. There is a massive anti-globalization movement of activists who interpret neo-liberal globalization as domination by political and economic elites, aligned with transnational capital and enforced by American and European militaries as a form of neocolonialism (Conway 2004; Santos 2006). This movement also encourages solidarity as an appropriate response to this threat.

The Christian churches have a long history of encouraging and responding to calls for global solidarity. For many years the churches organized nationally and ecumenically to support the struggle to end apartheid in South Africa (Pratt 1997). More recently, more than thirty Canadian churches and ecumenical organizations organized the Canadian Ecumenical Jubilee Initiative to campaign for the cancellation of unjustly accumulated debt by countries in the global south. Kairos is a Canadian ecumenical initiative formed in 2001 and built upon the thirty-year history of Canadian solidarity work in Africa, Asia, Latin America and the Pacific region and also with aboriginal communities (Cormie 2003; Lind & Mihevc 1994).

All of these are initiatives expressing global solidarity. This phrase has also changed meanings over time. Douglas Hicks quotes the work of the historian J.E.S. Hayward to point out that in nineteenth-century France the term was employed by different groups for quite different purposes. It was an appeal to unity but perhaps only among trade unions or only among the working classes. It was only later that the term began to be applied to "the need for *collective cooperation on the part of all persons and groups of society* to solve the complex social problems in a rapidly industrializing age" (Hicks 2000: 169). However, in Christian circles it has been developed on a universal basis as both a descriptive and normative quality including a preferential option for those suffering from deprivation, marginalization or oppression. "Solidarity can be understood as both a *descriptive* quality of actual societies and as a *normative* orientation, on the part of individuals, collectives, and policy-makers toward achieving such a (descriptive) social reality" (Hicks 2000: 171).

Solidarity, Sustainability, Sufficiency and Equity

Within the Christian understanding of solidarity, a question that has emerged is whether this virtue should apply only to human beings. If solidarity includes within it a preference for the weak and vulnerable, shouldn't the non-human aspects of Creation be included under the blanket of concern? Today the question of global climate change has emerged as the paradigmatic issue on which to test this and other questions of global ethics. For the Christian churches, though, the issue emerged before the question of climate change was on most people's agenda. The subject is now discussed using the language of ecojustice.

Ecojustice is a relatively new term in our lexicon, emerging only in the last forty years. Sometimes it is spelled with a hyphen (eco-justice) and sometimes without. It is widely used in the discourses of environmental studies, education and religion. It is increasingly used in philosophy and law. In this final section I want to trace the emergence of the term in ecumenical struggles among social and environmental activists. The relationship between these two justice-oriented groups had a dialectical character and the term ecojustice emerged as a synthesis of their competing claims.

The late 1960s was a time of great social and intellectual ferment. In North America the desire to address issues of social justice was strong and was reflected in political slogans like President Lyndon Johnson's "The Great Society" and Prime Minister Pierre Trudeau's "The Just Society." At the very same time there arose what came to be recognized as the ecological movement. This was concerned with pollution and the misuse of pesticides, as described for example in Rachel Carson's *Silent Spring* (1962). It also addressed the rapid increase in the world's population in the twentieth century, and the strain this was putting on the Earth's resources. One of the best examples of this was provided by the Club of Rome, an international think tank whose report *Limits to Growth* (Meadows et al.) was published in 1972.

Activists who focused on issues of poverty and racial injustice often advocated for economic policies that would encourage industrial growth in order to generate increased wealth. Concern for the environment was sometimes absent from this agenda. Activists who focused on issues of smog, birth control and endangered species often campaigned against industrial expansion in order to limit environmental damage. Concern for social inequality was often excluded from that agenda.

In the Christian churches both concerns were present but the focus on social justice was much stronger. In 1970 a U.S. Episcopal (Anglican) priest argued that "choosing [to work for] ecology instead of [against] poverty, or vice versa, is to make a bad choice"; the way ahead is to choose both (Faramelli 1970). Norman Faramelli was then working for the Boston Industrial Mission. At about the same time, a staff person for the American Baptist Churches named Richard Jones coined the term ecojustice "to mean both ecological wholeness and social justice" (Gibson 2004: 10 n12). The Presbyterian ethicist William Gibson describes ecojustice as recognizing "in other creatures and natural systems the claim to be respected and valued and taken into account in societal arrangements... The concern for ecological soundness and sustainability includes but transcends the concern of humans for themselves" (Gibson 2004: 34).

Since then the concept of ecojustice has been taken up by both religious and nonreligious voices. In the World Council of Churches a focus on a "just, participatory and sustainable society" was initiated at the 1975 Nairobi Assembly. From these discussions emerged the ethical norms of sustainability, sufficiency, participation and solidarity (Abrecht 1978). This was further developed at the Vancouver Assembly in 1983 with a focus on "Justice, Peace and the Integrity of Creation." The American ethicist Dieter Hessel (2007) describes the basic norms of ecojustice as follows:

- solidarity with other people and creatures—companions, victims, and allies—in earth community, reflecting deep respect for diverse creation;
- ecological sustainability—environmentally fitting habits of living and working that enable life to flourish, and utilize ecologically and socially appropriate technology;
- sufficiency as a standard of organized sharing, which requires

basic floors and definite ceilings for equitable or "fair" consumption;

- socially just participation in decisions about how to obtain sustenance and to manage community life for the good in common and the good of the commons.

Other authors have amended this last principle to describe it as the norm of equity, reinforcing the idea that ecojustice is inclusive of social justice. As we have seen earlier in this chapter, equity includes notions of fairness and is built upon a notion of moral equality but allows for differential treatment in order to achieve positive freedom. Some of these themes have been developed by the Lutheran theologian Larry Rasmussen in his *Earth Community, Earth Ethics* (1996; see also Hallman 2000). Several denominations have begun making explicit reference to the norms of sustainability, sufficiency, participation and solidarity,[8] and most recently we find Canadian ecumenical leaders calling on the Canadian government to ensure that its response to the economic crisis is shaped by the principles of solidarity, sustainability, sufficiency and equity.[9] In the Roman Catholic context, Pope John Paul II has called for an "ecological conversion" (Keenan 2002: 75). The development of ecojustice in other religious traditions has been chronicled in the multi-volume *Religions of the World and Ecology Series* edited by Mary Evelyn Tucker and John Grim.[10]

On the nonreligious side, the United Nations was key in promoting a series of events and reports that advanced the issue. In 1972 there was a UN conference in Stockholm on environment and development, and in 1983 the World Commission on Environment and Development was convened. It issued a report in 1987, by which time it had become known as the Brundtland Commission after its chair, Gro Harlem Brundtland. The report was titled *Our Common Future* (World Commission on Environment and Development 1987), and it focused on the concept of sustainable development, which it defined as "development that meets the needs of the present without compromising the ability of future generations to meet their own needs."

This was followed by a conference in Rio de Janeiro in 1992 that became known as the Earth Summit and again by a conference in Johannesburg in 2002 called Rio After Ten. The Earth Summit was significant for its Declaration, but also for what was not agreed upon. A draft declaration of Earth Rights was prepared, but there were not enough signatories for its adoption. In 1994 the former Soviet president Mikhail Gorbachev and the Canadian secretary-general of the Rio Earth Summit, Maurice Strong, revived the Declaration initiative with early support from the Government of the Netherlands. In 1997 they organized an independent Earth Charter Commission as a kind of people's movement. In 2000 the Earth Charter

"There is enough for everyone's need but not for everyone's greed." — Mahatma Gandhi

was officially launched, endorsed by nongovernmental groups and popular organizations around the world. The Earth Charter effectively elaborates the four ecojustice norms listed above (see earthcharter.org). A summary of the sixteen principles is attached in an appendix.

The Christian churches have endorsed the ethical principle of sustainability as a guide for the future, but have been critical of the narrowing of this principle to the concept of sustainable development. Instead the churches support the idea of sustainable community.[11] The concept of sustainable community draws attention to equitable relationships within human communities and also between humanity and the rest of Creation. It focuses on these relationships as the goal of economic development, not as a set of resources that exist to serve the economy.

Within this set of relationships the question of sustainability leads to the question of sufficiency. What is enough? Following on the above discussion of the common good, Christian churches have come to understand the provision of basic needs to be morally prior to the accumulation of excess, based on the concept of the preferential option for the poor. In addition, they have recovered from their spiritual traditions an understanding of restraint as a moral virtue, especially if it ensures the supply of basic needs (Hallman 2000). Using climate change as an example, the churches have argued that the Western nations responsible for the massive increase in atmospheric carbon dioxide from the Industrial Revolution on are also responsible for restraining their greenhouse gas emissions so that other nations might industrialize and overcome poverty.[12]

The tension between advocates of social justice and advocates for other communities of the Earth has not gone away. Campaigners for greater social equality remain concerned about what they see as attempts to restore ecological balance on the backs of the poorest people. At the same time, advocates of ecological integrity remain suspicious that attempts to address social inequality before environmental destruction, rather than both together, means that the rest of Creation remains fundamentally outside our intellectual and moral universe. As the German Protestant theologian Jurgen Moltmann put it:

> What we call the environmental crisis is not merely a crisis in the natural environment of human beings. It is nothing less than a crisis in human beings themselves. It is a crisis of life on this planet.... As far as we can judge, it is the beginning of a life and death struggle for creation on this earth. (Moltman 1985: xiii)

As the Canadian Catholic Bishops put it, "The cry of the earth and the cry of the poor are one" (Canadian Conference of Catholic Bishops 2003).

Examples of Ecojustice as Response to Globalization

Solidarity is one principle of ecojustice, but it is also an ethical concept drawn from struggles between people. After all, it's union members that sing "Solidarity Forever," isn't it? Another ecojustice principle is equity, and one of its meanings is socially just participation. How can we make sense of this in the environmental context?

Let's start with money. Canada's currency is closely tied to the value of our commodity exports. As oil reaches $100 per barrel, investors look at the profits being made in the oil patch and bid up the price of Canadian assets. This increases the pressure to eliminate barriers to resource exploitation. Profits are there to be made now. Ethical concerns for the state of Creation tomorrow aren't calculated as easily.

The logic of the oil patch also applies to the rising price of gold and other minerals. Mining often happens in remote regions and frequently on land whose title is disputed by indigenous peoples. For example, the Canadian company Goldcorp, owner of a gold mine in Red Lake, Ontario, currently operates a mine in Guatemala in defiance of the wishes of local indigenous communities. When Canadians express their solidarity with aboriginal groups in Canada or Central America, they are expressing their concern for social justice and environmental justice simultaneously.

One concern of the indigenous communities in Guatemala was over the use of cyanide in the mining process. This is also a concern of Canadians. Mining companies routinely use Canadian freshwater lakes as industrial waste dumps (called "tailings impoundment areas") for the disposal of toxic chemicals. According to Mining Watch (a Canadian non-for-profit environ-mental and social justice coalition), there are currently applications to engage in this activity in Sandy Pond, Newfoundland, Bucko Lake, Manitoba, and Fish Lake, British Columbia, along with ten other sites across the country. While current figures from the Canadian mining industry are not available, in 2005 the U.S. mining industry released 530 million kg of pollutants. The chemicals released in tailings and waste rock included almost 840,000 kg of cyanide, 1.6 million kg of mercury and 77 million kg of arsenic. This is what the Canadian Catholic Bishops mean when they say the cry of the Earth and the cry of the poor are one.

Let's take another example. This one comes from the fishery. I have identified indifference as one of the attitudes that allows a globalized ethic of competition to become an activity of domination. Well, decimation was the practice and indifference was the attitude of Euro-Canadians who eliminated the bison from the western Canadian prairie. We then applied industrial principles to the cod fishery on the Grand Banks with the same attitudes and results.

The common Friday dinner of fish and chips used to be made with cod and halibut. Now it's mostly made of pollock. More than 3 million tons of Alaska pollock is caught annually in the North Pacific, mostly in the Bering Sea. Half of it is caught by the U.S. fishing fleet using factory freezer trawlers. In addition to fish and chips you'll also find pollock in fish sticks, imitation crab meat, Chinese fish balls and many other fish formulations. If you choose the fish option at Dairy Queen, Arby's, Burger King or McDonald's, you'll probably end up eating pollock.

Since pollock can grow to over three feet in length and weigh over twenty kilos, you might wonder how it can be transformed into so many different shapes and flavours. The reason is because most pollock is made into surimi, a Japanese-style fish slurry. The fish is cleaned, rinsed to remove the smell and then pulverized into a gelatinous paste. It is then mixed with additives like starch, egg white, salt, vegetable oil, sorbitol and soy protein. Different seasonings are added depending on where in the world it will be eaten. In order to prevent it from spoiling in cold storage, sugar is added (up to 15 percent), which can make it a problem for diabetics. According to the U.S. Department of Agriculture, fish surimi contains 15 percent protein, 6.85 percent carbohydrate, almost no fat and 76 percent water (USDA National Nutrient Database).

Some people think we are being clever by finding new uses for fish species that we had ignored previously. On the other hand, the need for these new uses was created by a callous disregard for the consequences of current fishing practice.

Our search for new species leads to "fishing down the food web," because we are taking the food from the mouths of larger fish and mammals. This is causing all kinds of marine behaviour we have never seen before. Dolphins have been observed attacking seals for the first time. Killer whales have been feeding on otters.

Fishing down the food web means we are also taking the immature members of larger species, thus doubling the fatal consequences. Dr. David Pauly of the Fisheries Centre at the University of British Columbia likens this practice to "eating our seed corn." He argues that if we continue with the logic of feeding farther and farther down the food web, eventually we will be forced to figure out a way to turn plankton into surimi so we can make imitation varieties of all the fish species we used to have, but have no longer (Pauly 2005).

We are all part of the web of life—you, me, the salmon, cod, whales and kelp. We are all dependent on each other for oxygen, nutrients, food and life. If we continue our practice of decimation and indifference, eventually we will do to ourselves what we have done to the rest of Creation. We need to ask ourselves how implementing the ecojustice principles of sustainability, sufficiency, solidarity and equity would change this picture. Indifference has consequences.

For myself, I have become convinced that the developing concept of ecojustice can be a way forward, beyond the false dichotomy of social justice versus ecological justice, as long as it is understood as a term that can include both human suffering and the groaning of the Earth. One of the projects that has helped lead me to this conviction is the Earth Bible project from Australia (see Earthbible Website n.d.). Under the leadership of Dr. Norman Habel, a bible scholar from Flinders University in Adelaide, five volumes of essays have been published. These essays are by scholars the world over, all responding to six hermeneutical ecojustice principles. These are not ethical principles or principles of social organization. Rather they are principles for interpreting sacred texts. The use of these principles to guide biblical interpretation is an attempt to overcome the influence of other ideas, namely the separation of humanity from nature that was embedded in the eighteenth-century intellectual movement known as the Enlightenment.

Speaking as someone who comes to this debate after decades of involvement in social justice issues, I can say that the movement to an Earth-centred conciousness[13] is as profound a challenge as I have encountered. Working with the ecojustice principles of the Earth Bible Project has been helpful for understanding just how profound a challenge this is. Of course, adopting the language of ecojustice does not end all debates. It signals a profound shift in thinking and makes new solutions possible. Instead of thinking of the environment as merely the backdrop for the central human drama and a resource for its continuation, an ecojustice approach centres human life and activity within the web of all life and activity.

A formal secular definition of justice would be to give everyone that which is their due. In contemporary Christian theology, another way of thinking about justice is to understand it as "right relationship." An ecojustice approach understands right relationship in terms of all the communities of the Earth, giving all of them their due. It doesn't automatically resolve the question about the nature of these relationships, but it does suggest that all life has moral value and therefore can make claims on humans as moral agents (see Martin-Schramm & Stivers 2003). Again, from a Christian point of view, all Creation comes from God and all Creation bears the marks of God. Creation gives witness to the Creator (Acts 14:17) and makes plain God's power and nature (Rom 1:19–20). Right relationship is a foundational principle for all Creation, not just for humans. From this point on, no question of justice considered by humans can ignore the claims of the rest of Creation for right relationship.

Recently, a team of Quaker intellectuals tried to outline what a moral economy would look like, and their conclusion is that the fundamental paradigm of economics needs to be rethought (Brown & Garver 2009). Instead of a human or social economy, they argue, we need to build a whole earth economy, and this economy needs to be governed by and in the interest of right relationships. They encourage us to think of the human economy as a subset of the economy of the Earth, and not the other way around. In this they agree with Herman Daly and John Cobb Jr. They understand right relationship to be based on respect for all life, which they understand to be inherent in the Golden Rule and other ethical principles common to the great religious traditions of the world. They also imagine a set of economic arrangements that can determine when the economy has grown "enough." These are much more like ethical intimations than ethical principles, and they certainly have not been developed systematically. However, even in this short sketch it is possible to see how they may anticipate what I have described as the principles of ecojustice. They aim to achieve sustainability, and in their concern for an economy with an indicator of "enough" they allude to the ecojustice principle of sufficiency. They encourage solidarity among humans and between humans and the rest of Creation, and they are concerned for issues of fairness or equity.

Notes

1. This is partly attributable to the fact that the great thirteenth-century Dominican theologian Thomas Aquinas made it his life's work to integrate the philosophy of Aristotle with Christian theology. This was highly controversial in his day. His reputation increased over time, however, until in 1864 Pope Pius IX made him a teacher of the Church. Later Pope Leo XIII called his theology the definitive exposition of the Catholic faith.

2. "Then God said, 'Let us make humankind in our image, according to our likeness'" (Gen 1:26).

3. Young understands Thomas Spragens as saying that "the idea of the common good functions for the public reason of democracy as the ideal of truth functions in theoretical disciplines." See Spragens 1990: 120, quoted by Young 2000: 40.

4. The Dryden Chemicals pulp and paper mill stopped dumping mercury into the Wabigoon river system in northwestern Ontario in 1970. Forty years later the people of Grassy Narrows First Nation are still suffering the effects of mercury poisoning and still seeking compensation (see Paperny 2010).

5. Critical theory has also had an impact on Christian theology. See for example, Baum 1994.

6. Ignacio Ellacuria S.J. was a Spanish philosopher and university professor who was one of five Jesuit priests murdered, along with two employees, by the U.S.-trained army in San Salvador on November 16, 1989.

7. Young's model of democratic process is one of institutionalized and democratic

"struggle" (Young 2000: 52).

8. See for example, Presbyterian Eco-Justice Task Force, *Keeping and Healing the Creation*. Louisville: Committee on Social Witness Policy, Presbyterian Church (USA), 1989; Evangelical Lutheran Church in America. *Caring for Creation: Vision, Hope, and Justice*. Chicago: Division for Church and Society, 1993.

9. "Kairos Calls for a Moral response to the Economic Crisis," letter to the Canadian Prime Minister, the Provincial Premiers and the Leaders of Canada's Territories, January 23, 2009.

10. For more Christian reflection on sustainability see Rasmussen 1996 and Cobb 1992.

11. See the 1992 policy statement of the United Church of Canada "One Earth Community" at <united-church.ca/beliefs/policies/1992/o521>.

12. "In our vision of community, sufficiency is a key element—there is enough for all and all have enough. This vision includes physical, mental and spiritual health, food security in quantity and quality, clean air and water, good housing, educational opportunities, and adequate transportation. Relationships of justice and sufficiency produce a high degree of contentment, celebration and spiritual fulfillment that stands in marked contrast to the spiritual poverty of compulsive consumerism that is so much a part of many contemporary societies." David Hallman, "Report on the World Summit on Sustainable Development (WSSD)," World Council of Churches. Johannesburg, South Africa, August 26–September 4, 2002.

13. Some theologians refer to this as an Earth-centred pneumatology "that experiences God's spirit immanent in creation as the power of life-giving breath (*ruah*), the Wisdom (*logos*) continually working to transform and renew all life and the love that sustains it." Biblical images portray the Spirit as "a healing and subversive life-form—as water, light, dove, mother, fire, breath… wind." See Mark Wallace, "The Wounded Spirit as the Basis for Hope in an Age of Radical Ecology," in Hessel and Reuther 2000: 51–72.

Envisioning a Moral Economy

1773. That's what New Orleans 2005 reminds me of. In Cornwall, England, in 1773, a group of tin miners rioted. There was a shortage of wheat in the local market. Some local grain dealers had begun shipping Cornish wheat to the London market in order to profit from the higher prices instead of selling it locally. Seven or eight hundred miners went to the local grain merchant and offered 17 shillings for 24 gallons of wheat. When they were refused, they broke down the cellar doors and took the wheat without paying anything (Thompson 1971).

In 1766 the Sheriff of Gloucestershire described a similar scene. A mob had formed "consisting of the lowest of the people such as weavers, mecanicks, labourers, prentices, and boys etc…" They went first to the gristmill where they made off with the flour and wheat. Then they went to the local market where they set and enforced a lower price for grain. Finally they went to farmers, millers and bakers selling all manner of foodstuffs at prices they set, paying the owners according to those prices. In the words of the Sheriff, they "behaved with great regularity and decency where they were not opposed, with outrage and violence where there was: but pilfered very little" (Thompson 1991: 258).

Why does this remind me of New Orleans in 2005? Because in the examples above the common people were remembering and re-establishing a moral economy. They remembered that in times of mass hunger there were generally accepted moral principles that governed how people should behave. Prices should be fixed and the poor and hungry should be provided for. E.P. Thompson (1971) called this the "Moral Economy of the English Crowd."

When a father wades into a pharmacy looking for pop and diapers because tap water is unsafe to drink and babies need to be changed regardless, is it random lawlessness or responsible parenthood? When neighbours steal a van in order to evacuate a seniors' home abandoned by the civic authorities, is it theft or bravery? When local police break into a WalMart and set up camp, helping themselves to provisions, is it looting or setting public priorities over private ones? All of these are examples of reported behaviour by the residents of New Orleans in the aftermath of Hurricane Katrina. In each case their actions can be interpreted using two competing moral frameworks.

Part of the reaction around the world to the disastrous abandonment of the people of New Orleans by the U.S. federal government has to do with the apparent abandonment of moral principles by the highest authorities.

What ethical framework formed the foundation of their limited response? The conclusion of this book is that it was not the rejection of moral principles but rather the implementation of them. The American government was in the thrall of a neo-liberal ideology that endorsed economic globalization as the pathway to economic growth and well-being. Competitiveness was the new mantra and government was seen as an obstacle. The very real consequence of this globalization ethic was an activity of domination supported by an attitude of indifference. The members of the South End Press Collective described it this way:

> The lives of those who are poor, who are vulnerable, and who are not white are not valued by the U.S. government. And so, those with no means of escape were implored to pray and then blamed. And so, survivors were criminalized as "looters" for struggling to obtain food, water, diapers, medicine, and other essentials of life that no one else could or would provide. And so, they were left to die in prisons, in nursing homes, and on the street. (South End Press Collective 2007: vii)

Consider by contrast the reaction in Canada to the Red River flood of 1997. The rich were not rescued nor the poor left to drown. The influential were not fed while strangers starved. The healthy were not carried away while the sick were left to fend for themselves. All were treated equally because flood waters have no respect for social class. In 1997 students lined up to sandbag because everyone takes their turn. German soldiers training at CFB Shilo offered engineering and transportation assistance because they had the resources and Canadians had the need. When the people of St. Anne's prepared their curling rink to house evacuees, the fact that their neighbours were from the Roseau reserve was secondary. They were people first and members of different cultures second.

This is not an argument about Canada being better than the United States. Racism is alive and well north of the border, and the ethics of globalization are well entrenched. However, when the authorities down south dispatched military personnel to protect property instead of the poor, they violated some of the most deeply held moral values on both sides of the border. If you said to yourself, "This is not how a civilized country is supposed to behave!" you were echoing a memory going back hundreds of years. This memory is a memory of a moral economy, and it is a memory of a set of moral landmarks that form a kind of imaginary ethical enclosure. Within this enclosure a huge variety of political, economic, social and cultural arrangements will be accepted or tolerated. Outside of these boundaries, however, people will resist, protest, oppose and even rebel. This is true over time and also across cultures.

This book argues that there is a moral economy that exists as a coherent set of moral values embedded in strong communities. These values and commitments reveal themselves in times of crisis as guides for how to act when things are not normal. The public response to the flooding of the Red River Valley in 1997 is an example of these standards in action, when people were rescued according to need and not according to their class, status or ethnic background. The moral economy is also revealed by its absence, as when the state responded with indifference to the need of racialized minorities in the Katrina disaster of 2005.

I began with a historical review of how ethics became separated from economics at the level of formal discourse. Western culture historically had a suspicion of commerce and trade. The activity had been thought of as impure at least in part because it encourages the cultivation of impure (immoral) motives. Nowhere was this more developed than in discussions of usury. Economizing behaviour was well known and praised but commercial transactions were thought of as a subset of justice, so for centuries all economics was considered a subset of morality.

The language of political economy emerged in the sixteenth century as people began to examine wealth creation in terms of the actions of political states. The violent civil and religious struggles of this same period included the attempt to protect private property from interference by the church and then from interference by the state. By the eighteenth century this had the effect of separating business from government. Subsequently, the nineteenth century campaign against poverty and for wealth succeeded in separating economics from politics. Since politics is just another way of describing social ethics in practice, it was this same campaign that separated ethics from economics. The separation was a formal one, not intended to eliminate moral concern but rather to better serve it. The split seemed permanent when the discipline of economics took on the discipline of mathematics as its formal dialogue partner instead of the discipline of history. However, because this separation is morally grounded, it places arguments for and against it squarely within the field of moral discourse.

We continued the historical line in Chapter 2 by considering the work of the English historian E.P. Thompson. The identity of any society is maintained through collective memory and conveyed by culture. Thompson told the story of English villagers in the late eighteenth century who experienced sudden and dramatic changes to their customary lives. They defended their livelihoods by recalling an ancient moral consensus about how the community protects itself in times of famine and the roles played by the privileged and powerful. When those roles were abandoned, the people participated in direct action to defend their well-being.

The economic innovations they protested against were guided solely by the self-interest of those who stood to benefit from them. The innovations were defended by a new ideology that understood humans to be motivated solely by fear of starvation or unbridled greed—two conflicting appetites best adjudicated by unfettered market principles. The villagers judged this to be a poor guide to the common good.

They considered this a matter of justice because they remembered that, prior to the birth of modern economic thought, all behaviour, including economic behaviour, was believed to fall under the judgement of moralizing authorities like the king, the church and the conscience of the individual. Prior to the Industrial Revolution, economic relations in England were dominated by social relations. Thompson described this defence of common rights in this context as the moral economy of the English crowd. Thompson argued that the moral economy of the poor is summoned into being as a response to attacks on customary rights by the practice and ideology of the free market.

Through an examination of the work of Karl Polanyi we learned that when markets became linked they formed a market system, and it was this formation that caused the relationship between economy and society to be reversed. Economic relationships were disembedded from society and became something conceptually distinct called "the economy." When this happened economic norms began dominating social norms rather than the other way around. Society was thereafter refashioned to meet economic goals instead of the reverse. The political philosophy that endorsed this development was known as laissez-faire, meaning it advocated letting markets remain free from regulation.

Polanyi considered this political project to be disastrous, impossible and indeed utopian. It would not have happened spontaneously since "self-regulating" markets have to be created and maintained by the active intervention of political agents. In order for the linking of markets to be successful in forming a market system, Polanyi identified another set of changes that had to happen. Markets had to be created for three crucial factors—labour, land and money—since they were either not produced for sale, or not produced at all in the normal sense of that word.

The stark characterization of human behaviour as being governed by only two motives, hunger and gain, was true at that time only because it was made to be true. The social solidarity of the old order was abandoned in favour of a scientific approach thought to be as reliable as the principles governing the steam engine.

The utopian market economy is so threatening and destructive that it produces a reaction of social self-preservation. The whole process, taken together, is described by Polanyi as a double movement. This double movement includes an analysis of the economy as embedded in society. It is the disembedding of the economy that is experienced as dangerous and that forces a renewal of regulation in order to re-embed it. Attention to substantive economics is one way of reintroducing the texture of communal life into the discipline of formal economics.

The final implication of this analysis for our purposes is the recognition that all economies are embedded in institutions and social relations. There is no actually existing place called "the economy" governed by a logic and rationality all its own, as market liberals and some Marxists believe. People who advocate this line of thinking are those who try to persuade us that all our public policy choices must be limited by the need for consistency with market rationality.

On the contrary, all social structures have a moral character. So, in this sense we can say that all economies are moral economies. All economies are regulated by political processes or made possible by legal structures enforced by the state. Those processes and structures reflect a moral consensus among those with political power. We may consider that consensus illegitimate for any number of reasons (such as dictatorship, for example, or maldistribution of power through class, gender or racial oppression), but that doesn't mean there isn't a moral character to the economic arrangements. It only means that any particular moral economy might be considered immoral. This is probably the most important reason why so much debate on economic matters takes the form of a debate about justice.

To see how this concept of the moral economy operates in a different time and in different cultures, we then considered the work of the political scientist James C. Scott. In Scott's story of the village of Sedaka on the Muda plain of Malaysia, we also had a remembered village and a remembered economy. The villagers remembered when rents were paid after the harvest and were adjusted if the harvest was weak. They remembered the times before mechanization when harvest work was plentiful and everyone was always invited to the village feasts. They remembered in this way because they found themselves on the defensive as the market economy expanded and eroded the social contract on which their expectations rested. The social contract included the moral norms and cultural practices that constituted the moral economy. As the global spread of capitalist market economy becomes a universal experience, and as the moral economy becomes visible in the final stage of this historical process when ordinary people rise up to defend it, it becomes possible to describe some common principles of a moral economy. I have identified those four principles as sufficiency, sustainability, equity and solidarity.

The market failures that Thompson and Scott have described on a local scale were answered in the twentieth-century West by systems of national social insurance, or the welfare state. Since the fall of the Berlin Wall in 1989, this particular form of the moral economy has been under relentless attack by supranational organizations like the WTO. In response, peasant movements have increasingly turned to supranational cooperation, through vehicles like La Vía Campesina. Scott is sceptical that the supranational organization of farmers will be enough in the struggle to re-establish principles of moral economy, suggesting that a more powerful alliance might be formed by workers, remnants of the national bourgeoisie and the ballot box.

We learned from Polanyi and Thompson to interpret the appearance of a protest-based moral economy as the back half of the double movement: as social self-protection against the corrosive effects of the utopian, supposedly self-regulating, market system. Some authors have now taken this style of analysis in a new direction. Rather than restricting the concept of a moral economy to an ideal state of affairs or to moments of social protest, these authors conceive of the moral economy as a discipline of inquiry. This shift is based on the idea that the economy is *always embedded* in society and therefore the moral character of these economic relationships is always available for scrutiny. This represents a serious challenge to Polanyi's analysis. Does the presumption of an *always embedded economy* mean that the concept of the double movement is no longer credible?

Our answer is no. However, we have identified the need to flesh out the different meanings of embeddedness. The economy is an instituted process. All economies require institutions for their expression, even if the institution is the market. Institutions imply regulation whether these are formal, as in legal and political regulations, or informal, as in moral and cultural regulation. In this way we agree that all economies are embedded, meaning all economies require regulation of different kinds. We also agree that economies can be partly disembedded from regulatory regimes for limited periods of time.

In a separate meaning of embeddedness, we can also say that in market society the economy is disembedded from society because it has shifted from a dominant to a subordinate role in this relationship. The market economy can never become truly autonomous from society. However, because land, labour and money are now organized according to market principles, society is now subordinate to the market at the level of ideas.

Finally, because the economy is always embedded morally, it is possible to conceive of moral economy as a discipline of inquiry as well as a state of affairs. Any given economic activity may be embedded in a moral system we either currently support (voluntary blood donation) or find morally repugnant (slave labour), but the substantive economy remains embedded. However, where the market economy continues to expand we may find circumstances in which a market is partially embedded in law and politics, while at the same time being contested and therefore partially disembedded in morality and culture.

In Chapter 5 we considered contemporary experiences of marginalization and asked where these new forces were originating, and what had changed? The answer to this second question was economic and more specifically financial globalization. In this process of financial globalization, national financial markets have been linked together to form a single global market for credit, debt and currency. This global market has become either unregulated or insufficiently regulated because the corporations that dominate it are more powerful than the national governments that used to regulate them, and we have not yet invented the new global institutions that will be necessary for the regulation of this new market. For example, Fortis Bank was the largest retail bank in Belgium. It took three countries (Belgium, Luxembourg and Netherlands) to rescue it when it foundered in late September 2008. Iceland had to be rescued by the International Monetary Fund after its largest banks failed. The largest Icelandic bank had assets six times larger than the GDP of the whole country. It is doubtful that Switzerland could rescue UBS, which has assets 484 percent larger than that country's GDP. Credit Suisse is 290 percent larger than its home country's GDP, as is ING in relation to the Netherlands. Three of the five largest banks in the world are headquartered in the U.K. (RBS, HSBC and Barclays). Britain has already rescued Royal Bank of Scotland, but it probably couldn't rescue the other two single-handedly.

The corporate agents of the national financial sectors of our economies have become disembedded from the regulatory frameworks of the nation-state. They now exist in a new space called the globalized economy. It has now become so unstable and therefore so threatening to human society that even as prominent a champion of free-market capitalism as George W. Bush was prepared to nationalize portions of his banking sector to prevent further destruction.

When economic forces become disembedded from the restraints of the old society, there emerge champions of deregulation—let the market decide, they cry. In the late eighteenth century it was Adam Smith who argued that if everyone was simply left to pursue their own self-interest, these actions would be guided as if by "an invisible hand" to achieve the common good of wealth creation.

The social upheavals associated with the implementation of policies based on the rule of the invisible hand included market-induced famines, periodic shocks of industrial unemployment, dramatic increases in the gap between rich and poor, homelessness and waves of human migration as landless farmers sought to escape their poverty traps. William Blake described this in verse and Charles Dickens described it in prose.

In the late twentieth century, at the time of the globalization revolution, it was Milton Friedman who argued that markets freed from regulation were a precondition for human freedom in a modern society. We even had a wave of welfare reform in the 1990s to match the Poor Law reform of the 1830s, in both cases blaming the poor for their own condition.

The solution to the chaos caused by disembedded markets is obviously the re-embedding of those markets in new systems of political regulation. But what principles will guide this restructuring? Public protests against the bailouts of financial institutions that are too big or too interconnected to fail give some indication that business-as-usual is not an option.

In the last chapter we considered what those principles might be. An analysis of the ethics of globalization generated a contrast between an ethic of competition and an ethic of cooperation. The promotion of competition disconnected from other moral values leads to an activity of domination supported by an attitude of indifference. An ethic of cooperation generates an activity of solidarity supported by an attitude of compassion.

An examination of this typology revealed that it rested on a vision of the common good. Although this discourse has fallen from favour in much contemporary political theory, it has remained alive and developing in religious traditions. We considered how it has developed in Catholic theology, especially in response to a notion of tolerance that generates indifference instead of compassion. We also considered a contemporary critique of the concept of the common good generated by a political philosopher who wants to make space for difference, not on the basis of tolerance but on the basis of inclusion.

Finally, we examined how Christian churches have been engaged in practices of solidarity in the contemporary period and how that has led to the development of a set of ethical principles known as ecojustice. These principles are those of sustainability, sufficiency, solidarity and equity. While we have traced them briefly through the ideas of Christian thinkers, these principles are not exclusively Christian and can also be mapped in the documents of the United Nations and in other international declarations such as the Earth Charter.

This book is not intended to settle a question but to open up a discussion. Libraries are filled with debates about what constitutes a just society and right economic relations. I am not asking those questions. I am not even asking what is the most moral economy. Instead I am asking if there is a set of boundaries that enclose a diverse set of economic relations, all of which might be considered more or less moral, more or less just. I do not deduce this from first principles but rather pursue the logic that grows out of historical analysis and critical theory and that has found life in political economy, anthropology, sociology and ethics. I proposed four landmarks on these boundary lines. In the same way, I have not deduced these from some formula of logic. Instead I have identified principles that real institutions have used for real engagement with issues of injustice. There may be principles other than sustainability, sufficiency, solidarity and equity that belong on this list, and even those might be better expressed. However, I will not let the absence of a final answer get in the way of starting an important conversation. Insofar as ethics remains a part of public conversation, it is largely restricted to a discussion of duties and rumoured conflicts of interest. In order to organize an inquiry into, envision and generate support for a moral economy, we need to reanimate a public conversation about what constitutes a common good for all.

Appendix

Earth Charter Principles

1. Respect Earth and life in all its diversity.
2. Care for the community of life with understanding, compassion, and love.
3. Build democratic societies that are just, participatory, sustainable, and peaceful.
4. Secure Earth's bounty and beauty for present and future generations.
5. Protect and restore the integrity of Earth's ecological systems, with special concern for biological diversity and the natural processes that sustain life.
6. Prevent harm as the best method of environmental protection and, when knowledge is limited, apply a precautionary approach.
7. Adopt patterns of production, consumption, and reproduction that safeguard Earth's regenerative capacities, human rights, and community well-being.
8. Advance the study of ecological sustainability and promote the open exchange and wide application of the knowledge acquired.
9. Eradicate poverty as an ethical, social, and environmental imperative.
10. Ensure that economic activities and institutions at all levels promote human development in an equitable and sustainable manner.
11. Affirm gender equality and equity as prerequisites to sustainable development and ensure universal access to education, health care, and economic opportunity
12. Uphold the right of all, without discrimination, to a natural and social environment supportive of human dignity, bodily health, and spiritual well-being, with special attention to the rights of indigenous peoples and minorities.
13. Strengthen democratic institutions at all levels, and provide transparency and accountability in governance, inclusive participation in decision making, and access to justice.
14. Integrate into formal education and life-long learning the knowledge, values, and skills needed for a sustainable way of life.
15. Treat all living beings with respect and consideration.
16. Promote a culture of tolerance, nonviolence, and peace.

Bibliography

Abrecht, Paul (ed.). 1978. *Faith, Science and the Future*. Geneva: World Council of Churches.

Akturk, Sener. 2006. "Between Aristotle and the Welfare State: The Establishment, Enforcement, and Transformation of the Moral Economy in Karl Polanyi's *The Great Transformation*." *Theoria*, Apr. 1.

Andersen, Camilla. 2008. *Iceland Gets Help to Recover from Historic Crisis*. IMF Survey Online, December 2

Arnold, Thomas Clay. 2001. "Rethinking Moral Economy." *American Political Science Review* 95, 1 (March).

Atkinson, Anthony B. 2003. "Measuring Top Incomes: Methodological Issues." Unpublished paper.

Ayres, Clarence. 1935a. "Moral Confusion in Economics." *International Journal of Ethics* 45, January.

———. 1935b. "Discussion: Confusion Thrice Confounded." *International Journal of Ethics* 45, April.

Baldwin, John. 1959. "Medieval Theories of the Just Price: Romanists, Canonists, and Theologians in the Twelfth and Thirteenth Centuries." *Transactions of the American Philosophical Society* 49, Part 4: 14.

Bank for International Settlements (BIS). 2007. *Triennial Central Bank Survey of Foreign Exchange and Derivative Market Activity in April 2007*. Basel, Switzerland, September.

———. 1995. *Central Bank Survey of Foreign Exchange and Derivative Market Activity 1995*. Basel, Switzerland, May.

Barber, Bernard. 1995. "All economies are 'embedded': The career of a concept, and beyond." *Social Research*. 62/2 (Summer).

Bates, Robert H., and Amy Farmer Curry. 1992. "Community Versus Market: A Note on Corporate Villages." *American Political Science Review* 86, 2 (June).

Baum, Gregory. 1994. *Essays in Critical Theology*. Kansas City: Sheed & Ward.

BBC News. 2008. "U.K. Seeks Return of Iceland Cash." October 10.

Beaudin, Michel, and Guy Coté. 2002. "Le projet de zone libre-échange des Ameriques (ZLEA) mis en question par la tradition judéo-chrétiene," *Horizons Philosophiques* 13/1.

Berman, Bruce. 2007. "Moral Economy, Hegemony, Moral Ethnicity: The Cultural Politics of Modernity." Presented to the Ethnicity and Democratic Governance: Ethnic Claims and Moral Economies Workshop, Oxford, December 13/14.

Blackburn, Robin. 2008. "The Subprime Crisis." *New Left Review* 50 (March–April).

Block, Fred, and Karl Polanyi. 2003. "Karl Polanyi and the Writing of the Great Transformation," *Theory and Society* 32, 3 (June).

Block, Fred, and Margaret Somers. 1984. "Beyond the Economistic Fallacy: The Holistic Social Science of Karl Polanyi." In Theda Skocpol (ed.), *Visions and*

Methods in Historical Sociology. Cambridge: Cambridge University Press.

———. 2003. "In the Shadow of Speenhamland: Social Policy and the Old Poor Law," *Politics & Society* 31, 2 (June).

———. 2005. "From Poverty to Perversity: Ideas, Markets, and Institutions: Over 200 Years of Welfare Debate." *American Sociological Review* 70, 2 (April).

Bolton, Sharon C. 2009a "A Moral Modern Economy?" Work and Society Website, University of Strathclyde Business School.

———. 2009b "The Idea of a Moral Economy." Work and Society Website, University of Strathclyde Business School.

Bolton, Sir George. 1970. "Background and Emergence of the Eurodollar Market." In Herbert V. Prochnow (ed.), *The Eurodollar*. Chicago: Rand McNally.

Booth, Wayne. 1974. *Modern Dogma and the Rhetoric of Assent*. Chicago: University of Chicago Press.

Booth, William James. 1993. "A Note on the Idea of the Moral Economy." *American Political Science Review* 87, 4 (December).

———. 1994 "On the Idea of the Moral Economy." *American Political Science Review* 88, 3 (September).

Bourdieu, Pierre. 1998. *Acts of Resistance: Against the Tyranny of the Market*. Trans. by Richard Nice. New York: New Press.

Brown, Peter G., and Geoffrey Garver. 2009. *Right Relationship: Building a Whole Earth Economy*. San Francisco: Berrett-Koehler Publishers.

Burawoy, Michael. 2003. "For a Sociological Marxism: The Complementary Convergence of Antonio Gramsci and Karl Polanyi." *Politics & Society* 31, 2 (June).

Cangiani, Michele. 2008. "Polanyi's Institutional Theory of the Market System." Presented at the conference, The Relevance of Karl Polanyi for the 21st Century, Concordia University, December 9–11.

Carroll, K.W. 2007. "From Canadian Corporate Elite to Transnational Capitalist Class: Transitions in the Organization of Corporate Power." *Canadian Review of Sociology and Anthropology* 44, 3.

Carson, Rachel. 1962. *Silent Spring*. Boston: Houghton Mifflin.

Cassidy, John. 1999. "Time Bomb." *New Yorker* July 5.

CCA (Cooperative Association of Canada). nd. "Co-op Facts and Figures." <www.coopscanada.coop/en/about_co-operative/Co-op-Facts-and-Figures>.

Chattopadhyay, Paresh. 1974. "Political Economy: What's In a Name?" *Monthly Review* April.

CME Group. 2009. CME Group Volume Averaged 10.5 Million Contracts per Day in September 2009, Up 3 Percent from August 2009. <cmegroup.mediaroom.com/index.php?s=43&item=2937>.

Cobb, John B. Jr. 1992. *Sustainability: Economics, Ecology and Justice*. Maryknoll: Orbis Books.

Conway, Janet M. 2004. *Identity, Place, Knowledge: Social Movements Contesting Globalization*. Halifax: Fernwood.

Cooper, Richard N. 1997. "Review of Samuelson's *Economics: An Introductory Analysis*." *Foreign Affairs* Sept./Oct.

Cormie, Lee. 2003. "Ethics of Globalization." Paper presented at the Society of Christian Ethics Annual Meeting, Pittsburgh, PA. January.

Dale, Gareth. 2008. "Embeddedness and Decommodification: The 'Hard' and the 'Soft' Karl Polanyi." Presented at the conference, The Relevance of Karl Polanyi for the 21st Century, Concordia University, December 9–11.

Daly, Herman, and John Cobb Jr. 1994 [1989]. *For the Common Good*. Boston: Beacon Press.

Deane, Phyllis. 1978. *The Evolution of Economic Ideas*. Cambridge: Cambridge University Press.

Devine, Thomas M. 1994. *Clanship to Crofter's War: The Social Transformation of the Scottish Highlands*. Manchester: Manchester University Press.

Diamond, Barbara B., and Mark P. Kollar. 1989. *24-Hour Trading: The Global Network of Futures and Options Markets*. New York: John Wiley & Sons.

Drache, Daniel, and Wallace Clement (eds.). 1985. *The New Practical Guide to Canadian Political Economy*. Toronto: James Lorimer.

Dworkin, Ronald. 1985. *A Matter of Principle*. Cambridge, MA: Harvard University Press.

Earth Bible. n.d. *Reading the Bible from the Perspective of the Earth*. <webofcreation.org/Earthbible/earthbible.html>.

Eatwell, John, and Lance Taylor. 2000. *Global Finance at Risk: The Case For International Regulation*. New York: New Press.

Edelman, Marc. 2005. "Bringing the Moral Economy back in... to the Study of 21st-Century Transnational Peasant Movements." *American Anthropologist* September.

Ehrenreich, Barbara. 1989. *Fear of Falling: The Inner Life of the Middle Class*. New York: Harper Collins.

Elshtain, Jean Bethke. 1995. *Democracy on Trial*. New York: Basic Books.

Evans, Peter. 1995. *Embedded Autonomy*. Princeton: Princeton University Press.

Faramelli, Norman. 1970. "Ecological Responsibility and Economic Justice." *Andover Newton Quarterly* 11, Nov.

Fenlon, Brodie. 2009. "Mixed-use Condo to Replace 1 Bloor Project." *Globe and Mail* August 20.

Fourcade, Marion, and Kieran Healy. 2007. "Moral Views of Market Society." *Annual Review of Sociology* 33.

Frank, Robert H., Thomas Gilovich and Dennis T. Regan. 1993. "Does Studying Economics Inhibit Cooperation?" *Journal of Economic Perspectives* 7/2 (Spring).

Frieden, Jeffry A. 1987. *Banking on the World: The Politics of American International Finance*. New York: Harper & Row.

Gemici, Kurtulus. 2008. "Karl Polanyi and the Antimonies of Embeddedness." *Socio-Economic Review* 6: 5–33.

Gibson, William (ed.). 2004. *Eco-justice: The Unfinished Journey*. New York: SUNY Press.

Gilligan, Carol. 1982. *In a Different Voice*. Cambridge: Harvard University Press.

Gindon, Sam. 2002. "Social Justice and Globalization: Are They Compatible?" *Monthly Review* 54, 2 (June).

GLA Economics. 2009. "A Fairer London: The 2009 Living Wage in London." Greater London Authority. May.

Goodman, Michael K. 2004. "Reading Fair Trade: Political Ecological Imaginary and the Moral Economy of Fair Trade Foods." *Political Geography* 23, 7 (September).

Goodwin, G.B. 2008. "Reconsidering the Double Movement in the Age of Globalisation: The Case of Ecuador." Presented at the conference, The Relevance of Karl Polanyi for the 21st Century, Concordia University, December 9–11.

Granovetter, Mark. 1973. "The Strength of Weak Ties." *American Journal of Sociology* 78.

_____. 1985. "Economic Action and Social Structure: The Problem of Embeddedness." *The American Journal of Sociology* 91, 3 (November).

Gutmann, Amy, and Dennis Thompson. 1996. *Democracy and Disagreement*. Cambridge MA: Harvard University Press.

Hahn, F.H. 1987. "Review: *The Rhetoric of Economics* by Donald N. McCloskey." *Journal of Economic Literature* 25, 1 (March).

Hall, Peter, and David Soskice (eds.). 2001. *Varieties of Capitalism: The Institutional Foundations of Comparative Advantage*. Oxford: Oxford University Press.

Hallman, David G. 2000. *Spiritual Values for Earth Community*. Geneva: WCC Publications.

Hamilton, Adrian. 1986. *The Financial Revolution*. New York: Viking Penguin.

Hansen, Phillip. 1977. "T.H. Green and the Moralization of the Market." *Canadian Journal of Political and Social Theory* 1, 1 (Winter).

Hardaway, Donna. 1991. *Simians, Cyborgs, and Women*. New York: Routledge.

Hart, Keith. 2008. "'Economic Revolutions Are Always Monetary' (Mauss): Karl Polanyi and the Breakdown of the Neoliberal World Economy." Presented at the conference, The Relevance of Karl Polanyi for the 21st Century, Concordia University, December 9–11.

Hayward, J.E.S. 1959. "Solidarity: The Social History of an Idea in Nineteenth Century France." *International Review of Social History* 4/2.

Heath, Joseph 2009. *Filthy Lucre: Economics for People Who Hate Capitalism*. Toronto: HarperCollins.

Heilbroner, Robert. 1972. *The Making of Economic Society*. New Jersey: Prentice-Hall.

Hessel, Dieter T. 2007. "Eco-Justice Ethics." E-published by the Forum on Religion and Ecology, May 8.

Hessel, Dieter T., and Rosemary Radford Ruether (eds.). 2000. *Christianity and Ecology*. Cambridge, MA: Harvard University/Center for the Study of World Religions.

Hettne, Björn. 2008. "Development Discourses and Polanyian Transformations: A Renaissance of Development Studies?" Presented at the conference, The Relevance of Karl Polanyi for the 21st Century, Concordia University, December 9–11.

Heyward, Carter. 1982. *The Redemption of God: A Theology of Mutual Relation*. Lanham: University Press of America

Hicks, Douglas A. 2000. *Inequality & Christian Ethics*. Cambridge: Cambridge University Press.

Hirschman, Albert O. 1982. "Rival Interpretations of Market Society: Civilizing, Destructive or Feeble?" *Journal of Economic Literature* 20.

Hollenbach, David S.J. 2002. *The Common Good and Christian Ethics*. Cambridge: Cambridge University Press.

_____ 1986. "Economic Justice for All." Pastoral message from U.S. Conference of Catholic Bishops. < http://www.osjspm.org/economic_justice_for_all.aspx>.

Hutchinson, T.W. 1964. *'Positive' Economics and Policy Judgements*. London: George Allen & Unwin.

Jackall, Robert. 1988. *Moral Mazes: The World of Corporate Managers*. New York: Oxford University Press.

Johnson, Susan. 2008. "Polanyi and the Instituted Processes of Markets: Introducing a Wellbeing Perspective." Presented at the conference, The Relevance of Karl Polanyi for the 21st Century, Concordia University, December 9–11.

Karnitschnig, Matthew, and Deborah Solomon, Liam Pleven and Jon Hilsenrath. 2008. "U.S. to Take Over AIG in $85 Billion Bailout; Central Banks Inject Cash as Credit Dries Up." *Wall Street Journal* September 16.

Kerstetter, Steve. 2002. *Rags and Riches: Wealth Inequality in Canada*. Ottawa: Canadian Centre for Policy Alternatives

Kissinger, Henry. 1999. "Globalization and the World Order." Lecture delivered at Trinity College, Dublin. October 12.

Klein, Naomi. 2007. *The Shock Doctrine: the Rise of Disaster Capitalism*. Toronto: Knopf Canada.

Knight, Frank. 1935. "Intellectual Confusion on Morals and Economics." *International Journal of Ethics* January.

Knowles, Rob, and John R. Owen. 2008. "Karl Polanyi for Historians: An Alternative Economic Narrative." *The European Legacy* 13, 2 (April).

Kreiger, Andrew. 1992. *The Money Bazaar: Inside the Trillion-dollar World of Currency Trading*. New York: Times Books.

Krippner Greta R. 2001. "The Elusive Market: Embeddedness and the Paradigm of Economic Sociology." *Theory and Society* 30, 6 (December).

Krippner, Greta, R.M. Granovetter, F. Block, et al. 2004. "Polanyi Symposium: A Conversation on Embeddedness." *Socio-economic Review* 2.

Kroker, Arthur. 1977. "On Moral Economy." *Canadian Journal of Political and Social Theory* 1, 1 (Winter).

Lee, Kelley. 2004. "Globalisation: What Is it and How Does it Affect health?" *Medical Journal of Australia* 180 (4).

Lessig, Lawrence. 2009. *Remix: Making Art and Commerce Thrive in the Hybrid Economy*. Penguin: New York

Levitch, Richard, and Ingo Walter. 1989. "The Regulation of Global Financial Markets." In Theirry Noyelle (ed.), *New York's Financial Markets: The Challenges of Globalization*. Boulder, CO: Westview Press.

Lewis, Michael. 1989. *Liar's Poker*. New York: Viking Penguin.

Lind, Christopher, and Joe Mihevc (eds.). 1994. *Coalitions for Justice: Canadian Churches and Social Change*. Ottawa: Novalis.

Lind, Christopher. 1983. "Ethics, Economics & Canada's Catholic Bishops." *Canadian Journal of Political and Social Theory* VII, 3.

_____. 1995a. *Something's Wrong Somewhere: Globalization, Community and the Moral Economy of the Farm Crisis*. Halifax: Fernwood Publishing.

_____. 1995b. "How Karl Polanyi's Moral Economy Can Help Religious and Other Social Critics." In Kenneth McRobbie (ed.), *Humanity, Society and Commitment on Karl Polanyi*. Montreal: Black Rose

MacKenzie, Donald, and Yuval Millo. 2003. "The Historical Sociology of a Financial derivatives Exchange." *The American Journal of Sociology* 109, 1 (July).

Macleod, Angus. 1987 [1887]. "The Park Deer Raid November 22, 1887." *Glasgow Herald* Nov. 23. Angus Macleod Archive Online.

_____. 1888. "The Loch Crofters March to Lewis Castle in 1888." Angus Macleod Archive Online.

MacMurray, John. 1961. *Persons in Relation*. New York: Harper and Brothers.

Mahabharata Online. n.d. <www.mahabharataonline.com/translation/index. php>.

Maine, Henry. 1861. *Ancient Law*. London: John Murray.

Marable, Manning, and Leith Mullings (eds.). 2000. *Let Nobody Turn Us Around: Voices of Resistance, Reform, and Renewal*. Lanham, Maryland: Rowman and Littlefield.

Martin-Schramm, James B., and Robert L. Stivers. 2003. *Christian Environmental Ethics: A Case Method Approach*. Maryknoll, NY: Orbis Books,

Marx & Engels. 1959. *Basic Writings on Politics and Philosophy*. Lewis S. Feuer (ed.). Garden City, NY: Anchor Doubleday.

Marx, Karl. (1979). "Communist Manifesto." In Robert Tucker (ed.), *The Marx-Engels Reader*. New York: Norton.

Mauss, Marcel. 1925. *The Gift*. London: Cohen and West.

McCloskey, D.N. 1983. "The Rhetoric of Economics." *Journal of Economic Literature* XXI.

_____. 1985. *The Rhetoric of Economics*. Madison: University of Wisconsin.

McQuaig, Linda. 2001. *All You Can Eat*. Toronto: Penguin.

Meadows, Meadows, Randers & Behrens. 1972. *Limits to Growth*. Rome: Club of Rome.

Migone, Andrea. 2008. "Embedded Markets: A Dialogue between F.A. Hayek and Karl Polanyi." Presented at the conference, The Relevance of Karl Polanyi for the 21st Century, Concordia University, December 9–11.

Moltmann, Jurgen. 1993 [1985]. *God in Creation*. Minneapolis: Fortress Press.

Myrdal, Gunnar. 1969. *Objectivity in Social Research*. New York: Pantheon.

NCBA (National Cooperatives Business Association). nd. "About Cooperatives." <www.ncba.coop/abcoop_stats.cfm>.

Norton, Wayne. 1994. *Help Us to a Better Land: Crofter Colonies in the Prairie West*. Regina: Canadian Plains Research Centre.

Nussbaum, Martha C. 2000. *Women and Human Development: The Capabilities Approach*. Cambridge: Cambridge University Press.

Ó Riain, Seán. 2006. "Time–Space Intensification: Karl Polanyi, the Double Movement, and Global Informational Capitalism." *Theory and Society* 35.

O'Brien, David J., and Thomas A. Shannon (eds.). 1992. *Catholic Social Thought*. Maryknoll, NY: Orbis Books.

Ohnuki-Tierney, Emiko. 1993. *Rice as Self*. Princeton, NJ: Princeton University Press.

Oliver, Edward 2008. "A Chronology of the London Living Wage Campaign." Dept. of Geography, Queen Mary University of London, December.

Orlando, Giovanni. 2008. "(Re)Approaching through Complexity Polanyi's Embeddedness in Anthropology: An Ethnographic Example from Contemporary Sicily." Presented at the conference, The Relevance of Karl Polanyi for the 21st Century, Concordia University, December 9–11.

Owen, John R. 2007. "The Moral Economy of Saint Thomas Aquinas: Agent

Sovereignty, Customary Law and Market Convention." *The European Legacy* 12, 1 (February).

Palacios, Juan José. 2001. "Globalisation's Double Movement: Societal Responses to Market Expansion in the 21st Century." Paper prepared for the proceedings of the Eighth Karl Polanyi International Conference "Economy and Democracy." Universidad Nacional Autónoma de México, Mexico City, November 14–16.

Paperny, Anna Mehler. 2010. "Decades-old Mercury Poisoning Shown to have Lasting Effect on Native Community." *Globe and Mail* April 6

Parsons, Talcott, and Neil Smelser. 1984 [1956]. *Economy and Society.* London: Routledge & Kegan Paul.

Paton, Joy. 2008. "Polanyian Pedagogy: Political Economy and the Praxis of Transformation." Presented at the conference, The Relevance of Karl Polanyi for the 21st Century, Concordia University, December 9–11.

Pauly, Daniel. 2005. "The Ecology of Fishing Down Marine Webs." *Society for Conservation Biology Newsletter* 12/4, November.

Perry, Ralph Barton. 2007 [1909]. *The Moral Economy*. New York: Charles Scribner's Sons (republished as an ebook by Project Gutenberg).

Pfanner, Eric. 2008. "Iceland Is all but Officially Bankrupt." *New York Times*, Oct. 9.

Piketty, Thomas 2003. "Income Inequality in France, 1901–1998." *Journal of Political Economy* 111 (5).

Piketty, Thomas, and Emmanuel Saez. 2003. "Income Inequality in the United States, 1913–98," *Quarterly Journal of Economics* 118 (1).

Polanyi, Karl. 1947. "Our Obsolete Market Mentality." *Commentary* 3/2 (February).

_____. 1957 [1944]. *The Great Transformation*. Boston: Beacon Press.

_____. 2001 [1944]. *The Great Transformation*. "Foreword" by Joseph Stiglitz; "Introduction" by Fred Block. Boston: Beacon Press.

Polanyi, Karl, Conrad M. Arensberg and Harry W. Pearson. 1957. *Trade and Market in the Early Empires*. New York: The Free Press

Polanyi-Levitt, Kari. (ed.). 1990. *The Life and Work of Karl Polanyi*. Montreal: Black Rose Books.

Pollin, R., and S. Luce 1998. *The Living Wage: Building a Fair Economy*. New York: New Press.

Porter, Michael. 1990. *The Competitive Advantage of Nations*. New York: Free Press.

Powelson, John P. 1998. *The Moral Economy*. Ann Arbor: The University of Michigan Press.

Pratt, Renate. 1997. *In Good Faith: Canadian Churches Against Apartheid*. CSSR, Waterloo: Wilfred Laurier University Press

Putnam Robert. 1993. *Making Democracy Work: Civic Traditions in Modern Italy*. Princeton: Princeton University Press.

Ramsay, Meredith. 1996. *Community, Culture, and Economic Development: The Social Roots of Local Action*. Albany: State University of New York Press.

Rasmussen, Larry. 1996. *Earth Community, Earth Ethics*. Maryknoll, NY: Orbis Books.

Rawls, John. 1987. "The Idea of Overlapping Consensus." *Oxford Journal of Legal Studies* 7.

Redfield, Robert. 1960. *The Little Community and Peasant Society and Culture*. Chicago: University of Chicago Press.

Robinson, Joan. 1963. *Economic Philosophy*. Chicago: Aldine.

Rodik, Dani. 2008. *The Death of the Globalization Consensus*. Project Syndicate, July 25, 2008.

Rotstein, Abraham. 1986. "The Reality of Society: Karl Polanyi's Philosophical Perspective." Paper presented to the Karl Polanyi Commemorative Conference, Hungarian Academy of Sciences, Budapest, Oct.; published in Kari Polanyi-Levitt. 1990. *The Life and Work of Karl Polanyi* Montreal: Black Rose Books.

Ruggie, John G. 1982. "International Regimes, Transactions, and Change: Embedded Liberalism in the Postwar Economic Order." *International Organization* 36, 2 (Spring).

Sailing Networks. 2006. "Amazing Story of Mike Golding and Alex Thomson in the Velux 5 Oceans." <www.sailingnetworks.com/news/read/5131>.

Saez, Emmanuel, and Michael R. Veall. 2005. "The Evolution of High Incomes in North America: Lessons from Canadian Evidence." *The American Economic Review* 95, 3 (June).

Samuelson, Paul. 1983 [1947]. *Foundations of Economic Analysis*. Cambridge: Harvard University Press.

Sanger, David E. 2009. "Nationalization Gets a New, Serious Look." *New York Times* January 25.

Santos, Boaventura de Sousa. 2006. *The Rise of the Global Left: The World Social Forum and Beyond*. London: Zed Books.

Sayer, Andrew. 2004. "Moral Economy." Dept. of Sociology, Lancaster University.

_____. 2005 *The Moral Significance of Class*. Cambridge: Cambridge University Press.

_____. 2006. "Approaching Moral Economy." In Nico Stehr, Christoph Henning & Bernd Weiler (eds.), *The Moralization of the Markets*, New Brunswick, NJ: Transaction Publishers.

_____. 2007. "Moral Economy and Employment." In Sharon C. Bolton and Maeve Houlihan (eds.), *Searching for the Human in Human Resource Management*, Basingstoke, U.K.: Palgrave Macmillan.

_____. Undated. "Moral Economy." Department of Sociology, Lancaster University, Lancaster LA1 4YL, U.K.

Scarboro Missions. n.d. Golden Rule Poster. < http://scarboromissions.ca/Golden_rule/poster_order.php>.

Schwab, Klaus. 2009. "The Competitiveness Report 2009–2010." World Economic Forum, Geneva.

Scott, James C. 1976. *The Moral Economy of the Peasant*. New Haven: Yale University Press.

Scott, James C. 1977. "Protest and Profanation: Agrarian Revolt and the Little Tradition, Part I." *Theory and Society* 4, 1 (Spring).

_____. 1985. *Weapons of the Weak*. New Haven: Yale University Press.

_____. 1990. *Domination and the Arts of Resistance*. New Haven: Yale University Press.

_____. 2005. "Afterword to 'Moral Economies, State Spaces, and Categorical Violence.'" *American Anthropologist* September, 107: 3.

Sen, Amartya. 1985. *Commodities and Capabilities*, Oxford: Oxford University Press

Serageldin, Israel. 1995. *Sustainability and the Wealth of Nations: First Steps in an Ongoing Journey*. Washington, DC: The World Bank Environmentally Sustainable Studies and Monograph Series, No. 5.

Shah, Hetan, and Martin McIvor (eds.). 2006. *A New Political Economy*. London: Compass in association with Lawrence & Wishart.

Silver, Beverly J., and Giovanni Arrighi. 2003. "Polanyi's 'Double Movement': The Belle Époques of British and U.S. Hegemony Compared." *Politics & Society* 31, 2 (June).

Sklair, L. 2001. *The Transnational Capitalist Class*. Oxford: Blackwell.

Social Affairs Commission, Canadian Conference of Catholic Bishops. 2003. "Pastoral Letter on the Christian Ecological Imperative." Ottawa: CCCB.

Solow, Robert. 2001. "1935 Where We Were—Where We Are 2000." In Jeff E. Biddle, John B. Davis and Steven G. Medema (eds.), *Economics Broadly Considered: Essays in Honor of Warren J. Samuels*. London: Routledge.

South End Press Collective. 2007. *What Lies Beneath: Katrina, Race, and the State of the Nation*. Cambridge, MA: South End Press.

Spragens, Thomas. 1990. *Reason and Democracy*. Durham, NC: Duke University Press.

Stearns, Peter. 1998. *The Industrial Revolution in World History*. Boulder, CO: Westview Press.

Steiner, Philippe. 2009. "Who Is Right About the Modern Economy: Polanyi, Zelizer, or both?" *Theory and Society* 38.

Tawney, R.H. 1920. *The Acquisitive Society*. New York: Harcourt, Brace and Howe.

_____. 1937 [1926]. *Religion and the Rise of Capitalism*. Harmondsworth, U.K.: Penguin Books.

_____. 1931 [1952]. *Equality*. Fourth edition. London: George Allen & Unwin. 4th edition.

_____. 1983. "Poverty as an Industrial Problem." In J. Atherton (ed.), *The Scandal of Poverty*. Mowbray.

Taylor, Charles. 1989. *Sources of the Self: The Making of the Modern Identity*. Cambridge MA: Harvard University Press.

Tett, Gillian. 2009. *Fool's Gold*. New York: Free Press.

The Economist. 2008. "Suffering a Seizure: America's Government Takes Control of Freddie Mac and Fannie Mae." September 8.

Thompson, E. P. 1971. "Moral Economy of the English Crowd." *Past And Present* 50.

_____. 1978. "Eighteenth-Century English Society: Class Struggle without Class?" *Social History* 3, 2 (May).

_____. 1991. *Customs in Common*. New York: The Free Press.

Thompson, William, and Joseph Hickey. 2005. *Society in Focus*. Boston, MA: Pearson.

Thrupp, Sylvia. 1942. *The Merchant Class in Medieval London*. Chicago, IL: University of Chicago Press.

Titmuss Richard. 1971. *The Gift Relationship*. New York: Pantheon.

Toronto Community Foundation. 2009. "Vital Signs 2009." Toronto Community Foundation, October.

Tucker, Mary Evelyn, and John Grim, eds. 1997–2004. *Religions of the World and Series*. Cambridge: Center for the Study of World Religions, Harvard Divinity School, distributed by Harvard University Press.

Twin, Alexandra. 2008. "Stocks Crushed." <CNNMoney.com> September 29.

Vecsey, George. 2008. "A Sporting Gesture Touches 'Em All." *New York Times* April 30.

Vezér, Erzsébet. 1990. "The Polanyi Family." In Kari Polanyi-Levitt (ed.), *The Life and Work of Karl Polanyi*. Montreal: Black Rose Books.

Wakamori, Fumitaka. 2008. "'Habitation versus Improvement' in the Age of a Knowledge-based Economy." Presented at the conference, The Relevance of Karl Polanyi for the 21st Century, Concordia University, December 9–11.

Walton, John. 1992. *Western Times and Water Wars: State, Culture and Rebellion in California*. Berkeley: University of California Press.

Walzer, Michael. 1983. *Spheres of Justice*. New York: Basic Books.

Washington Post. 2004. "As Income Gap Widens, Uncertainty Spreads." September 19.

Wearden Graeme, and Phillip Inman. 2008. "Northern Rock Repays £2bn of £26bn Bank of England Loan." *The Guardian* January 11.

Weber, Max. 1976 [1958]. *The Protestant Ethic and the Spirit of Capitalism*. New York: Charles Scribner's Sons.

Welch, Sharon D. 2000. *A Feminist Ethic of Risk*. Minneapolis: Augsburg Fortress.

Williams, Richard C. 2007. *The Cooperative Movement: Globalization from Below*. Burlington, VT: Ashgate Publishing.

Williamson, John. 2000. "What Should the World Bank Think About the Washington Consensus?" *World Bank Research Observer* 15, 2, (August). Washington, DC: The International Bank for Reconstruction and Development.

Wills, J., N. Kakpo, R. Begum 2009 "Is There a Business Case for the Living Wage? The Story of the Cleaning Service at Queen Mary, University of London." Dept. of Geography, University of London, January.

Wjuniski, Bernardo Stuhlberger, and Ramón García Fernández. 2008. "Polanyian Lessons For Our Days: The Case Of Brazil." Presented at the conference, The Relevance of Karl Polanyi for the 21st Century, Concordia University, December 9–11.

World Commission on Environment and Development. 1987. *Our Common Future*. Oxford: Oxford University Press.

Yalnizyan, Armine. 2007. *The Rich and the Rest of Us: The Changing Face of Canada's Growing Gap*. Ottawa: Canadian Centre for Policy Alternatives, March.

Young, Iris Marion. 2000. *Inclusion and Democracy*. Oxford: Oxford University Press.

Zedillo, Ernesto. 2006. "Give Globalization a Hand." *Forbes Magazine* September 19.

Zelizer, Viviana. 1994. "The Creation of Domestic Currencies." *The American Economic Review* 84, 2 (May).

Zelizer, Viviana. 2000. "Fine Tuning the Zelizer View." *Economy and Society* 29/3.

_____. 2008. "The Real Economy." *Qualitative Sociology* June 31, 2.

Zukin, Sharon, and Paul DiMaggio (eds.). 1990. *Structures of Capital: The Social Orgaization of the Economy*. Cambridge: Cambridge University Press.